THE LITTLE
BOOK OF
BANANAS

HQ
An imprint of HarperCollins*Publishers* Ltd
1 London Bridge Street
London SE1 9GF

www.harpercollins.co.uk

HarperCollins Publishers
1st Floor, Watermarque Building, Ringsend Road, Dublin 4, Ireland

This edition 2021

1
First published in Great Britain by
HQ, an imprint of HarperCollins*Publishers* Ltd 2020

ISBN: 978-0-00-849181-9

Book Design: Steve Wells

MIX
Paper from
responsible sources
FSC™ C007454

This book is produced from independently certified FSC™ paper
to ensure responsible forest management.

For more information visit: www.harpercollins.co.uk/green

Printed and bound in Italy by Rotolito S.p.A.

THE LITTLE BOOK OF BANANAS

SALLY EL-ARIFI

HQ

An imprint of HarperCollinsPublishers Ltd.

CONTENTS

MUFFINS, BISCUITS AND TEA TIME TREATS

DESSERTS AND PUDDINGS

SAVOURY DISHES

INTRODUCTION

Bananas are greatly important around the world. Every part of a banana is used in some way, from the fibres for fabric in Japanese culture, the sap in fabric dye to the leaves for cooking – the whole plant has many uses. Most well known, of course, is eating it.

I can still remember sitting on the counter while my mother recounted each step of banana bread to me. I was six and it was the first cake that I learnt how to bake. She measured everything by eye and I guess I absorbed the skill by watching her. This was when I fell in love with food and this love of food led me to specialize in food science and nutrition at university. I wanted to really understand the science behind the ingredients used in baking. It is this knowledge, in addition to my professional experience as a chef, baker and chocolatier, that you can take advantage of throughout this book. It is my fervent aim to help chefs and bakers of all levels to learn more about the food we eat and how we can use ingredients in unexpected ways to create something amazing.

Later in life, when I turned my craft to baking, I tried to apply the same freehand attitude in my mother's cooking to my work and I failed miserably. Invigorated by my botched experiments, I threw myself into the science of it all. Although my soap-tasting experiments weren't always appealing (do not overdo it on the baking powder), I was able to couple my instinct to craft like my mother with applying the chemistry of baking to create some of my best recipes. You see, relying solely on instinct wasn't enough when it came to baking; my recipes needed the order, the structure of science to back it up.

In the middle of my journey, I may have fallen out of love with bananas briefly. Banana-flavoured medicine was something I, like many children, had to endure when I was unwell, which had left a long-lasting sour taste in my mouth, forever associating banana flavouring with being off school and re-runs of daytime TV. Eventually, I wanted to rediscover the love of bananas I once had but because there were very few banana-centric recipes out there, I needed to start multiple recipes from the ground up, which was a lot of fun. Thankfully, as time passed, I came to love the fruit again.

Bananas are incredibly underrated. They have such varying characteristics, from green to brown, and can bring something unique and amazing to any sweet or savoury recipe. To create this book, I expanded my already vast collection of banana recipes to really take advantage of the fruit's versatility.

The first time I realized that you could cook the banana peel was incredibly exciting for me. Not only did it reduce food waste, but it was a new ingredient to try. My taste testers (my family) had to deal with some very interesting flavour combinations and textures but when the recipes worked, it was a great triumph.

Bananas also represent so much more than flavour for me. The fruit touches on my Ghanaian, Sudanese and British heritage, from tatale (plantain pancakes) to banana bread. This book is a collection of all the banana recipes that I have created over the years and I am so happy to be able to share them with you. I've added some tips to particular recipes that welcome creative flair.

TRAFFIC LIGHT BANANAS

A banana has a large variety of properties during its life. From green to black, the starches in the fruit transform into sugars, changing not only its appearance but its taste and texture as well. At the top of each recipe, it will tell you which colour and ripeness of banana is needed and best used.

GREEN

At the green stage, bananas have a higher starch to sugar ratio and so are very useful for savoury dishes. They have a potato-like texture and don't have a very strong taste so are ideal for soaking up flavours.

YELLOW

This is the stage that most people enjoy eating bananas. Bananas at the yellow stage have a good balance of sugars and starch which makes them ideal for smoothies and certain cake recipes.

BROWN

This is when bananas are reaching the end of their life, but fear not! At this stage they are great for cakes and pancakes. They can also be used as an egg replacement in certain recipes, making them a useful vegan ingredient.

BLACK

Black bananas may not be very appealing but black plantains are delicious and can be used for all sorts of dishes. Black plantains can be fried, turned in to delicious fritters and a whole lot more.

GLOSSARY OF BAKING TERMS

UK	US
baking parchment	parchment paper
baking tray	cookie sheet
bicarbonate of soda	baking soda
biscuit	cookie
cake tin	cake pan
caster sugar	superfine sugar
choux pastry	cream puff paste
clingfilm	plastic wrap
coriander	cilantro
cornflour	cornstarch
dark chocolate	bittersweet chocolate
demerara sugar	turbinado sugar
desiccated coconut	shredded dried coconut
digestive biscuit	graham cracker
double cream	heavy cream
flapjacks	granola bars
frying pan	skillet
full-fat milk	whole milk
ginger nut biscuit	ginger snap
golden syrup	light corn syrup
ground almonds	almond flour

UK	US
icing	frosting
icing sugar	confectioner's sugar
lolly	popsicle
muscovado sugar	brown sugar
palette knife	metal spatula
pepper	bell pepper
piping bag	pastry bag
plain flour	all-purpose flour
porridge oats	rolled oat
pudding	dessert
scone	biscuit
self-raising flour	self-rising flour
semi-skimmed milk	low-fat milk
sieve	strain
single cream	light cream
sponge finger	lady finger
tin, tinned	can, canned
tea towel	dishcloth
wire rack	cooling rack

CAKES, LOAVES & TRAYBAKES

BANANA BREAD

Prep Time 10–15 minutes
Cook Time 50 minutes–1 hour
Serves 8–10
Type of banana: BROWN
Nut Free

200g (7oz) salted butter, softened
100g (3½oz) light brown sugar
100g (3½oz) caster sugar
2 eggs, beaten
2 large bananas, mashed
200g (7oz) self-raising flour
1 tsp baking powder

Preheat the oven to 200°C/180°C fan/400°F/Gas 6.

Grease a 1kg (2lb) loaf tin and line the base and sides with baking parchment.

Beat the butter and both sugars together until light and fluffy.

Gradually add the eggs. If the mixture begins to split at this point, add a tablespoon of the flour to bring it back together.

Mix in the mashed banana.

Sift in the flour and baking powder and then fold the batter until fully combined.

Pour into the prepared tin and bake for 50 minutes–1 hour until a skewer comes out clean when the cake is poked in the middle. Cool in the tin before enjoying.

Tip: The loaf can be frozen for up to 1 month. Just wrap it tightly in clingfilm before freezing.

DATE AND PORT LOAF

Prep Time 25–30 minutes

Cook Time 1 hour 10 minutes–1 hour 20 minutes

Serves 8–10

Type of banana: BROWN

Nut Free

180g (6¼oz) dates, pitted and chopped
130ml (4½ fl oz) boiling water
3½ tbsps port
80g (2¾oz) salted butter, softened
150g (5¼oz) light brown sugar
1 large banana, mashed
1 egg, beaten
180g (6¼oz) plain flour
1 tsp bicarbonate of soda
2 tsps baking powder

Preheat the oven to 170°C/150°C fan/325°F/Gas 3.

Grease a 1kg (2lb) loaf tin and line the base and sides with baking parchment.

Soak the dates in the boiling water for 10 minutes. Once they have softened, blend with an electric mixer until smooth, and stir in the port.

In a separate bowl, beat the butter and sugar together until fluffy. Beat in the banana and egg until combined.

Fold in the flour, bicarbonate of soda and baking powder and then stir in the blended date mixture. Pour into the prepared tin.

Bake for 1 hour 10 minutes–1 hour 20 minutes until a skewer comes out with only a few moist crumbs when the loaf is poked in the middle. Remove from the oven and cool completely in the tin.

Tip: This loaf can be tightly wrapped in clingfilm and frozen for up to 1 month if, for some reason, you can't eat it fast enough!

FRUIT AND NUT LOAF

Prep Time 20–25 minutes
Cook Time 30–40 minutes
Serves 8–10
Type of banana: YELLOW
Dairy Free | Vegan

50g (1¾oz) hazelnuts,
 roughly chopped
60g (2oz) dried apricots, diced
50g (1½oz) currants
135ml (4½ fl oz) water
2 tbsps sunflower oil
80g (2¾oz) caster sugar
1 tsp bicarbonate of soda
1 large banana, diced
110g (4oz) plain flour
Zest of 1 orange
1 tsp vanilla extract
½ tsp ground cinnamon

Preheat the oven to 180°C/160°C fan/350°F/Gas 4.

Grease a 1kg (2lb) loaf tin and line the base and sides with baking parchment.

Put the hazelnuts, apricots, currants, water, oil and sugar in a saucepan and simmer over a low heat for 2 minutes. Pour the hot fruit and nut mix into a large heatproof bowl and whisk in the bicarbonate of soda and diced banana. Fold in the flour, orange zest, vanilla and cinnamon until fully combined.

Pour the mix into the prepared tin and bake for 30–40 minutes until a skewer comes out clean when the loaf is poked in the middle.

Remove from the oven and allow to cool completely in the tin.

Tip: If you want to save this loaf for later, you can wrap it tightly in clingfilm and keep it in the freezer for up to 1 month.

MARBLED BANANA BREAD

Prep Time 20–25 minutes
Cook Time 55 minutes–1 hour 5 minutes
Serves 8–10
Type of banana: BROWN
Nut Free

170g (6oz) salted butter, softened
170g (6oz) caster sugar
3 eggs, beaten
2 large bananas, mashed
170g (6oz) self-raising flour
1 tsp baking powder
1 tbsp cocoa powder

FOR THE ICING
100g (3½oz) icing sugar
1 tbsp water

Preheat the oven to 180°C/160°C fan/350°F/Gas 4.

Grease a 1kg (2lb) loaf tin and line the base and sides with baking parchment.

Beat the butter and sugar together until pale and fluffy. Beat in the eggs. Mix in the mashed banana, flour and baking powder.

Separate about one-third of the banana batter into a separate bowl and fold the cocoa powder into it. Pour one-third of the banana batter into the prepared loaf tin. Add the chocolate banana batter and then the final third of the banana batter on top of this so you have three layers. Using a knife, swirl the layers together to create a marble effect.

Bake for 55 minutes–1 hour 5 minutes until a skewer comes out clean when it is poked in the middle. Allow the cake to cool in the tin.

Sift the icing sugar and mix with the water until smooth. Drizzle over the cooled cake.

Tip: This delicious banana bread is best eaten in its first few days of freshness – if it even lasts that long.

BANANA HONEY BREAD

Prep Time 10–15 minutes

Cook Time 55 minutes–1 hour 5 minutes

Serves 6–8

Type of banana: BROWN

Nut Free

120g (4¼oz) salted butter, softened
100g (3½oz) caster sugar
2 tbsps runny honey
2 eggs, beaten
225g (8oz) self-raising flour
2 medium bananas, mashed
½ tsp lemon juice

Preheat the oven to 180°C/160°C fan/350°F/Gas 4.

Grease a 1kg (2lb) loaf tin and line the base and sides with baking parchment.

Beat the butter, sugar and honey together until fully combined. Add the eggs, flour, mashed banana and lemon juice and mix until smooth.

Spoon the mixture into the prepared loaf tin and bake for 55 minutes–1 hour 5 minutes until golden brown and a skewer comes out clean when it is poked in the middle.

Allow to fully cool in the tin before slicing and enjoying.

Tip: Eat this loaf at its best, within 2–3 days of being baked.

FUN FACT

It is thought that bananas originated in Indonesia, the Philippines or New Guinea between the years 8000 and 5000 BCE.

PEANUT BUTTER AND CHOCOLATE BANANA BREAD

Prep Time 15–20 minutes

Cook Time 55 minutes–1 hour

Serves 8

Type of banana: BROWN

Dairy Free | Vegan

---

3 bananas

150g (5¼oz) peanut butter

6 tbsps maple syrup

6 tbsps vegetable oil

6 tbsps dairy-free milk

1 tbsp vanilla extract

250g (8¾oz) plain flour

80g (2¾oz) light brown sugar

1 tsp baking powder

½ tsp bicarbonate of soda

¼ tsp salt

100g (3½oz) dark chocolate, chopped

Preheat the oven to 180°C/160°C fan/350°F/Gas 4.

Grease a 1kg (2lb) loaf tin and line the base and sides with baking parchment.

Mash 2 bananas with 100g (3½oz) of the peanut butter, then add the maple syrup, oil, milk and vanilla extract. Add all the dry ingredients and fold until fully combined.

Pour the mixture into the prepared tin and then dot the remaining peanut butter on top. Roughly swirl the peanut butter into the batter with a knife and then smooth the top of the mixture with a spatula. Cut the remaining banana in half vertically down its length and place the halves on top of the loaf, cut side facing up.

Bake the loaf for 55 minutes to 1 hour until a skewer comes out clean, with just a few moist crumbs, when it is poked in the middle. Check the loaf at around 30 minutes and if the top is golden brown, place a layer of foil over the top of the loaf to avoid burning.

Remove from the oven and allow to completely cool in the tin.

Tip: This loaf doesn't really freeze well because of the peanut butter but it only lasts 1 day in my house so I'm sure it'll go quickly.

SPICED BANANA LOAF

Prep Time 10–15 minutes
Cook Time 55 minutes–1 hour 5 minutes
Serves 8
Type of banana: BROWN
Nut Free

180g (6¼oz) dates, pitted and chopped
180ml (¾ cup) boiling water
80g (2¾ oz) salted butter, softened
150g (5¼oz) caster sugar
1 large egg, beaten
1 banana, mashed
180g (6¼oz) plain flour
1 tsp bicarbonate of soda
2 tsps baking powder
1 tsp ground cinnamon
½ tsp ground nutmeg
½ tsp ground ginger

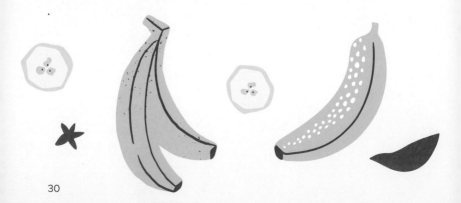

Preheat the oven to 180°C/160°C fan/350°F/Gas 4.

Grease a 1kg (2lb) loaf tin and line the base and sides with baking parchment.

Soak the dates in the boiling water for 10 minutes, then blend with a electric mixer until smooth.

In a separate bowl, beat the butter and sugar together until smooth. Beat in the egg and banana. Fold in the flour, bicarbonate of soda, baking powder, cinnamon, nutmeg and ginger. Add the date mixture and stir until fully combined.

Spoon into the prepared tin. Bake for 55 minutes–1 hour 5 minutes until a skewer comes out with only a few moist crumbs when the loaf is poked in the middle. Remove from the oven and cool completely in the tin.

Tip: This loaf keeps its freshness for longer (for over 4 days) because it is so moist. Store in an airtight container to keep it soft.

BANANA AND WALNUT CRUMBLE CAKE

Prep Time 25–30 minutes
Cook Time 30–40 minutes
Serves 8–10
Type of banana: BROWN

FOR THE WALNUT CRUMBLE
10g (⅓oz) salted butter
1 tbsp light brown sugar
1½ tbsps plain flour
10g (⅓oz) walnut halves, crushed

FOR THE CAKE
70g (2½oz) salted butter, softened
175g (6oz) light brown sugar
2 large bananas
2 eggs
½ tsp vanilla extract
200g (7oz) self-raising flour
1 tsp bicarbonate of soda
½ tsp salt

FOR THE ICING
100g (3½oz) cream cheese
1 tsp vanilla extract
50g (1¾oz) icing sugar

Preheat the oven to 180°C/160°C fan/350°F/Gas 4.

Grease the base and sides of two 20cm (8in) round cake tins, and line with baking parchment.

To make the crumble, put the butter, sugar and flour in a bowl and rub together with your fingertips to form crumbs. Once there are no large lumps of butter, add the walnuts. Set aside for later use.

To make the cake, beat the butter and sugar together until pale and fluffy. In a separate bowl, mash the bananas, eggs and vanilla together. Gradually add the banana mixture to the butter and sugar. Sift the flour, bicarbonate of soda and salt into the mixture and fold until fully combined. Evenly divide the cake mixture between the prepared tins.

Sprinkle the walnut crumble on top of both cakes and then bake for 30–40 minutes until the cakes are golden brown and spring back when gently pressed. Allow them to cool in the tins for 15 minutes before removing and placing on a wire rack.

For the icing, whisk the cream cheese and vanilla together with an electric mixer until smooth. Gradually sift in the icing sugar and then whisk on high speed for around 2 minutes until thick.

Once the cakes are cool, spread the icing on top of one of the cakes. Place the other cake on top, crumble side up.

Tip: Try replacing the walnuts in the crumble with different nuts or dried fruit – for example hazelnuts or apricots work well.

BANANA CHRISTMAS CAKE

Prep Time 25–30 minutes + overnight soaking + 2–3 months maturing + 30 minutes decorating
Cook Time 3 hours
Serves A lot of people!
Type of banana: YELLOW

200g (7oz) dried apricots
250g (8¾oz) dried figs
400g (14oz) prunes
250g (8¾oz) sultanas
5 tbsps brandy
300g (10½oz) salted butter, softened
200g (7oz) dark brown sugar
5 eggs
2 bananas, mashed
2 tbsps molasses or treacle
Zest of 2 oranges
1 tsp ground cinnamon
1 tsp ground ginger
½ tsp ground nutmeg
580g (1lb 4oz) plain flour
Brandy, for soaking

FOR THE MARZIPAN AND ICING
4 tbsps marmalade, warmed
Icing sugar, for dusting
455g (1 lb) white marzipan
2 tbsps brandy
1kg (2lb) sugar paste icing

TO DECORATE (OPTIONAL)
Candied fruit (see Tip)
Cinnamon sticks
Star anise

Cut the apricots, figs and prunes into small pieces and place with the sultanas and brandy in a medium saucepan. Bring to the boil and then pour into a large, heatproof bowl. Cover the bowl with clingfilm and leave to steep overnight in the fridge.

Preheat the oven to 170°C/150°C fan 325°F/Gas 3.

Grease the base and sides of a deep 23 x 18cm (9 x 7in) cake tin and line with baking parchment.

Beat the butter and sugar together in a large bowl until pale and fluffy. Add the eggs one at a time, mixing between each addition. Stir in the mashed banana, molasses or treacle and orange zest. Sift the cinnamon, ginger, nutmeg and flour into the batter and fold until combined.

Stir in the soaked fruit and then spoon the cake batter into the prepared tin and smooth the top with a palette knife.

Bake for 3 hours until a cake skewer comes out clean with only a few crumbs. Remove from the oven and wrap the cake in foil while still warm to keep it moist.

Keep the cake wrapped tightly in foil and store in an airtight cake tin for 2–3 months. Once a week, poke a few holes in the top of the cake and spoon over 1–2 tablespoons of brandy. This will help keep it moist and the flavour will develop and mature.

Continued overleaf

Scientists believe that
bananas were the first fruit to
ever be cultivated, but they
were only considered globally
popular in the 20th century.

One week before the cake is required, brush the top with the warmed marmalade. Dust the work surface and a rolling pin with icing sugar and roll out the marzipan to the shape and size of the cake and then carefully place the marzipan over the cake. Smooth out the marzipan, ideally with an icing smoother but you can use your hands dusted with icing sugar. Trim off any excess and then allow to dry for 1 or 2 days.

Brush the marzipan surface with the brandy. Dust the work surface with icing sugar and roll out the icing to around 1.5cm (¾in) thickness. Carefully cover the cake with the icing and then smooth it to remove any lumps and bumps.

Decorate with candied fruit, cinnamon sticks and star anise as desired.

After all your hard work with this cake, make sure you keep it in an airtight container, and it will keep for over a month. You can even freeze it and it'll stay delicious for a year, just make sure you wrap it tightly in clingfilm to stop the sugar paste from weeping.

TIP: To make the candied fruit, slice 2 oranges, lemons or satsumas into rounds about 2.5mm (⅛in) thick. Mix 250g (8¾oz) caster sugar with 250ml (1 cup) water in a frying pan over a medium heat. When the mixture starts to boil, drop in your fruit slices one at a time. Continue to cook the fruit slices over medium heat until the pith turns translucent (about 20 minutes), turning them over occasionally. Continue cooking for a further 10 minutes over a low heat until they are tender but still intact. Take the pan off the heat and carefully remove the fruit to a wire rack. Dry the slices on the rack for around 2 days and then store in an airtight container.

HUMMINGBIRD CAKE

Prep Time 20–25 minutes
Cook Time 25–30 minutes
Serves 8–10
Type of banana: YELLOW

200g (7oz) self-raising flour
200g (7oz) caster sugar
½ tsp salt
¼ tsp baking powder
½ tsp ground nutmeg
1 tsp ground cinnamon
2 eggs, beaten
150ml (5 fl oz) vegetable oil
1 tsp vanilla extract
1 large banana, mashed
100g (3½oz) tinned pineapple, drained and roughly chopped
50g (1¾oz) pecan nuts, roughly chopped

FOR THE ICING
200g (7oz) cream cheese
60g (2oz) unsalted butter, softened
1 tbsp runny honey
140g (5oz) icing sugar
½ tsp vanilla extract
½ tsp salt

TO DECORATE
Edible flowers and leaves
Pecan nuts

Preheat the oven to 180°C/160°C fan/ 350°F/Gas 4.

Grease the base and sides of two 20cm (8in) round cake tins and line with baking parchment.

Mix together the flour, sugar, salt, baking powder, nutmeg and cinnamon in a large bowl. Add the eggs and oil, stirring until dry ingredients are mostly combined.

Stir in the vanilla, mashed banana, chopped pineapple and chopped pecans.

Divide the batter evenly between the prepared tins and bake for 25–30 minutes until a skewer comes out clean when inserted in the centre of the cakes.

Leave the cakes to cool in the tins for about 15 minutes then remove from the tins and leave to cool completely on a wire rack.

For the icing, beat the cream cheese, butter and honey with an electric mixer on medium–low speed until smooth. Gradually sift in the icing sugar, beating on low speed until blended after each addition. Stir in the vanilla. Increase the speed to medium–high and beat for about 2 minutes until the mixture is thick and holds its shape.

Place one cake on a serving platter and spread half of the icing on top. Place the second cake on top and spread the remaining icing on top of this. Decorate with the edible flowers and pecans.

Tip: Use colourful edible flowers such as pansies and marigolds to give your cake the wow factor.

BANANA RUM CAKE

Prep Time 25–30 minutes
Cook Time 35–40 minutes
Serves 8–10
Type of banana: BROWN
Dairy Free | Vegan | Nut Free

---

2 tsps vanilla extract
100g (3½oz) vegan margarine, softened
250g (8¾oz) demerara sugar
280g (10oz) self-raising flour
Pinch of salt
½ tsp baking powder
1 large banana, mashed
180ml (¾ cup) dairy-free milk
5 tbsps spiced rum

FOR THE ICING
50g (1¾oz) icing sugar
2 tsps light rum

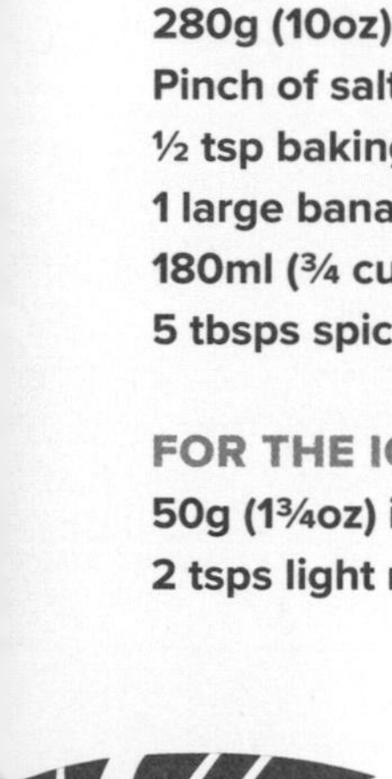

Preheat the oven to 180°C/160°C fan/350°F/Gas 4.

Grease a 25cm (10in) bundt tin by brushing melted margarine or oil into every nook and cranny.

In a large bowl, beat together the vanilla, margarine and demerara sugar until there are no lumps of margarine left. Add the rest of the ingredients and beat together until smooth.

Pour the batter into the prepared cake tin and bake for 35–40 minutes. Remove the cake from the oven and allow it to cool for 15 minutes in the tin before turning onto a wire rack.

Once the cake is completely cool, sift in the icing sugar, mix together with the rum until smooth. Drizzle the icing over the cake.

Tip: I sometimes dust the inside of the tin with flour after greasing it if I am using a tin with lots of creases.

You can use any kind of rum that you want in this recipe. I use spiced rum because it gives the cake a richer flavour.

CHOCOLATE ESPRESSO CAKE

Prep Time 25–30 minutes
Cook Time 30–35 minutes
Serves 8–10
Type of banana: YELLOW
Nut Free

200g (7oz) plain flour
250g (8¾oz) caster sugar
15g (½oz) cocoa powder
Pinch of salt
½ tsp bicarbonate of soda
½ tsp baking powder
2 tbsps instant coffee
1 small banana, mashed
150ml (5 fl oz) semi-skimmed milk
120ml (1/3 cup) water
1 tsp vanilla extract
150ml (5 fl oz) sunflower oil
50g (1¾oz) dark chocolate, plus chocolate shavings to decorate

FOR THE FROSTING
1 tbsp boiling water
2 tbsps instant coffee
100g (3½oz) salted butter, softened
400g (14oz) cream cheese
280g (10oz) icing sugar

Preheat the oven to 180°C/160°C fan/350°F/Gas 4.

Grease the base and sides of two 20cm (8in) round tins and line with baking parchment.

In a large bowl, mix the flour, sugar, cocoa powder, salt, bicarbonate of soda, baking powder and coffee.

Place the banana, milk, water, vanilla, oil and chocolate in a saucepan and warm over a low heat, stirring the mixture occasionally to stop the chocolate from burning. Once the chocolate has melted, add the mixture to the dry ingredients and beat until smooth and fully combined.

Bake for 30–35 minutes, then remove from the oven and allow to cool completely in the tin.

For the frosting, mix the boiling water and instant coffee together in a small bowl until the coffee has fully dissolved.

In a separate bowl, beat the butter for about 2 minutes until there are no lumps and it is fluffy. Add the cream cheese and beat again for a further minute. Gradually sift in the icing sugar and beat until it is fully combined. Fold in the coffee.

Place one of the cooled cakes on a serving platter and spread one-third of the icing on top. Place the second cake on top, then spread the rest of the icing on top and around the edges of both cakes. Decorate with chocolate shavings.

BLACK VELVET CAKE

Prep Time 15–20 minutes

Cook Time 30–35 minutes

Serves 8–10

Type of banana: BROWN

Nut Free

150g (5¼oz) salted butter, softened
260g (9oz) light brown sugar
2 small bananas, mashed
1 egg
225g (8oz) self-raising flour
1½ tsps white wine vinegar
½ tsp bicarbonate of soda
50g (1¾oz) cocoa powder, plus extra for dusting
225ml (7½ fl oz) Guinness

FOR THE FROSTING
200g (7oz) cream cheese
150g (5¼oz) icing sugar

Preheat the oven to 180°C/160°C fan/350°F/Gas 4.

Grease and line the base and sides of two 20cm (8in) round tins with baking parchment.

Beat the butter and sugar together until fluffy with no lumps of butter. Mix the rest of the cake ingredients into the butter and sugar and beat until smooth.

Pour the mixture into the prepared tins and bake for 30–35 minutes until a skewer comes out clean when inserted in the centre of the cakes.

Remove from the oven and leave to cool in the tins for 15 minutes before sliding onto a wire rack to cool completely (the cakes can sink slightly when they come out the oven, but there's no need to worry).

To make the frosting, whip the cream cheese and icing sugar together for around 2 minutes until thick. Spread half of this on top of one of the cooled cakes. Place the other cake on top and spread the remaining frosting on top. Dust with cocoa powder and enjoy.

Tip: Add some chocolate shavings to the top of the cake to give it a little extra something.

PIÑA COLADA CAKE

Prep Time 30–35 minutes
Cook Time 15–20 minutes
Serves 8–10
Type of banana: YELLOW
Nut Free

200g (7oz) self-raising flour
200g (7oz) caster sugar
½ tsp salt
¼ tsp baking powder
2 eggs, beaten
150ml (⅔ cup) vegetable oil
1 tsp vanilla extract
100g (3½oz) tinned pineapple, drained and roughly chopped
1 banana, mashed
40g (1½oz) desiccated coconut, plus extra to decorate

FOR THE BUTTERCREAM ICING
150g (5¼oz) salted butter, softened
250g (8¾oz) icing sugar
3 tbsps coconut rum
5 drops yellow gel food colouring
Tinned pineapple, cubed, to decorate

Preheat the oven to 180°C/160°C fan/350°F/Gas 4.

Grease the base and sides of two 20cm (8in) round cake tins and line with baking parchment.

Mix together the flour, sugar, salt and baking powder in a large bowl. Add the eggs and oil, stirring until the dry ingredients are mostly combined.

Stir the vanilla, chopped pineapple, mashed banana and desiccated coconut into the mixture.

Divide the batter evenly between the two prepared tins and bake for 15–20 minutes until a skewer comes out clean when inserted in the centre of the cakes.

Leave the cakes to cool in the tins for 15 minutes then remove from the tins and leave to cool completely on a wire rack.

For the buttercream icing, beat the butter with an electric mixer on medium–low speed until smooth. Gradually sift in the icing sugar, beating on low speed until blended after each addition. Beat the butter and icing sugar on medium–high speed for around 2 minutes until fluffy and pale. Stir in the rum and then beat for a further 30 seconds. Fold in the yellow food colouring so you are left with a marbled buttercream.

Place one cooled cake on a serving platter and spread one-third of the icing on top. Place the second cake on top and spread the rest of the icing on top and around the edges of the cake. Decorate with cubes of pineapple and desiccated coconut.

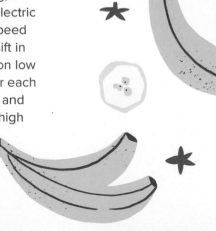

CHOCOLATE AND HAZELNUT MICROWAVE MUG CAKE

Prep Time 5 minutes
Cook Time 2½–3½ minutes
Makes 1
Type of banana: BROWN
Gluten Free

---

1 medium banana
1 tbsp sunflower oil
1 egg
1 tbsp semi-skimmed milk
4 tbsps caster sugar
3 tbsps buckwheat flour
1 tbsp cocoa powder .
¼ tsp gluten-free baking powder
Pinch of salt
2 tbsps chopped hazelnuts, plus extra (optional) to top
Whipped cream, to serve (optional)

FOR THE GANACHE
1 tbsp double cream, plus 2 tbsps to top (optional)
30g (1oz) milk chocolate

Grease a 350ml (1½ cup) mug.

In a bowl, mash the banana with the oil, egg and milk until smooth. Add the sugar, flour, cocoa powder, baking powder and salt and mix until fully combined. Fold in the chopped hazelnuts and then pour the mixture into the greased mug.

Cook in the microwave for 2 minutes 40 seconds at 1000W, 3 minutes at 800W or 3 minutes 20 seconds at 600W. Leave to cool completely before decorating. If the cake rapidly sinks when the microwave stops, microwave for a further 15 seconds, but slight shrinkage is normal.

While the cake is cooling, make the chocolate ganache by microwaving the cream and chocolate in 15-second bursts. Stir the chocolate after every 15 seconds until it is fully melted. Whisk together until fully combined and then allow to cool slightly to become firmer. When the cake is cool pour the ganache over the top. For extra indulgence, top the cake with whipped cream and extra chopped hazelnuts, if you like.

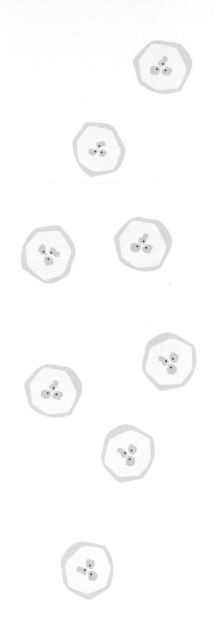

BERRY SQUARES

Prep Time 30–35 minutes
Cook Time 30–35 minutes
Serves 12
Type of banana: YELLOW
Dairy Free | Nut Free | Vegan

180g (6¼oz) frozen mixed berries
2 tbsps caster sugar
80ml (¼ cup) boiling water
80g (2¾oz) vegan margarine, softened
150g (5¼oz) caster sugar
1 banana, mashed
180g (6¼oz) plain flour
2 tsps baking powder
1 tsp bicarbonate of soda
¼ tsp salt
Handful of fresh blueberries, strawberries or raspberries, to decorate

FOR THE BUTTERCREAM FROSTING
100g (3½oz) vegan margarine, softened
1 tsp vanilla extract
125g (4½oz) icing sugar

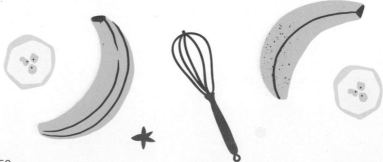

Preheat the oven to 180°C/160°C fan/350°F/Gas 4.

Grease the base and sides of a 20 x 25cm (8 x 10in) rectangular tin and line with baking parchment.

Add the berries to a bowl, sprinkle in the sugar and pour in the boiling water, then set aside for 10 minutes to allow the berries to soften before roughly blending using a stick blender until the mixture is mostly smooth.

In a bowl, beat the margarine and sugar together until pale and fluffy. Fold in the banana, flour, baking powder, bicarbonate of soda and salt. Fold the blended berry mix into the cake batter then pour into the prepared cake tin.

Bake for 30–35 minutes until a skewer comes out mostly clean with only a few moist crumbs when inserted in the centre of the cake. Allow to completely cool in the tin.

To make the buttercream frosting, beat the margarine and vanilla extract with an electric mixer for 2 minutes. Gradually sift in the icing sugar. Beat all the ingredients together for another 2 minutes on high speed until fluffy.

Slide the cake out of the tin once completely cool. Spread the buttercream on top of the cake and then slice into 12 equal squares. Decorate each square as desired with some fresh berries.

FUN FACT

The bananas enjoyed today are very different from the original wild crop. The original fruit contained a number of large, hard seeds with a very small amount of edible flesh.

BANANA AND PECAN TRAYBAKE

Prep Time 10–15 minutes

Cook Time 30–35 minutes

Serves 8

Type of banana: YELLOW

Dairy Free | Vegan

240g (8½oz) caster sugar
100g (3½oz) vegan margarine, softened
1 tsp vanilla extract
1 large banana, mashed
250ml (1 cup) non-dairy milk
280g (10oz) self-raising flour
½ tsp salt
1 tsp ground cinnamon
50g (1¾oz) pecan nuts, chopped, plus extra to decorate

Preheat the oven to 200°C/180°C fan/400°F/Gas 6.

Grease the base and sides of a 20 x 25cm (8 x 10in) rectangular tin and line with baking parchment.

In a large bowl, beat together the sugar, margarine, vanilla and banana until smooth. Add the milk, flour, salt and cinnamon and mix until fully combined. Fold in the pecans and then pour into the prepared tin.

Sprinkle the extra chopped pecans over the top of the mixture. Bake for 30–35 minutes until a skewer comes out mostly clean when it is poked in the middle.

Remove from the oven, allow to cool in the tin and then cut into 8 equal pieces.

HAZELNUT BROWNIES

Prep Time 10–15 minutes
Cook Time 1 hour 5 minutes
Makes 16
Type of banana: YELLOW
Dairy Free | Vegan

200g (7oz) plain flour
250g (8¾oz) light brown sugar
15g (½oz) cocoa powder
Pinch of salt
½ tsp bicarbonate of soda
½ tsp baking powder
50g (1¾oz) hazelnuts, chopped
1 banana, mashed
250ml (1 cup) non-dairy milk
1 tsp vanilla extract
150ml (⅓ cup) sunflower oil
50g (1¾oz) dark chocolate

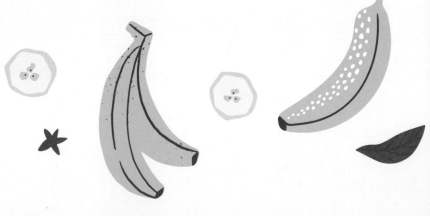

Preheat the oven to 180°C/160°C fan/350°F/Gas 4.

Grease the base and sides of a deep 23 x 18cm (9 x 7in) baking tray and line with baking parchment.

In a large bowl, mix the flour, sugar, cocoa powder, salt, bicarbonate of soda, baking powder and chopped hazelnuts.

Place the banana, milk, vanilla, oil and chocolate in a saucepan and warm over a low heat. Make sure to stir the mixture occasionally to stop the chocolate from burning. Once the chocolate has melted, add to the dry ingredients and beat until smooth and fully combined. Pour the batter into the prepared baking tray.

Bake for 35 minutes and then switch off the oven. Leave in the cooling oven for a further 30 minutes. Remove from the oven and allow to cool completely before cutting into 16 equal pieces.

Tip: You can swap the hazelnuts for any kind of nut, or dried fruit such as cranberries, you wish.

CHOCOLATE BROWNIES

Prep Time 20–25 minutes
Cook Time 40–45 minutes
Makes 9
Type of banana: YELLOW
Nut Free

175g (6oz) salted butter, softened
180g (6¼oz) dark chocolate
1 tsp vanilla extract
3 eggs, beaten
225g (8oz) light brown sugar
2 small bananas, mashed
175g (6oz) plain flour
60g (2oz) white chocolate chips (optional)

Preheat the oven to 180°C/160°C fan/350°F/Gas 4.

Grease the base and sides of a 20cm (8in) square tin and line with baking parchment.

Melt the butter and chocolate together in a microwave in 30-second bursts, stirring in between each burst. Once melted, set aside.

Mix the vanilla, eggs and sugar together until just combined. Gradually add the melted chocolate and butter to the eggs and sugar. Mix till smooth. Add the mashed banana, flour and chocolate chips, if using, and mix till just combined.

Pour into the prepared tin and bake for 40–45 minutes – there should still be a slight wobble in the middle. Remove from the oven and allow to cool completely in the tin. Remove from the tin and cut into 9 equal pieces. Enjoy!

Tip: You can replace the white chocolate chips with chopped nuts such as pecans or dried fruit such as apricots.

The change, from the original wild bananas to the current popular fruit, occurred around CE 650 in Africa. Two varieties, Musa acuminata and Musa balbisiana, were crossbred which created the seedless bananas that we see today.

BLONDIES

Prep Time 20–25 minutes
Cook Time 45–50 minutes
Makes 9
Type of banana: YELLOW
Nut Free

175g (6oz) salted butter
140g (5oz) white chocolate
3 eggs, lightly beaten
1 tsp vanilla extract
100g (3½oz) caster sugar
125g (4½oz) light brown sugar
2 small bananas, mashed
175g (6oz) plain flour
60g (2oz) white chocolate chips (optional)

Preheat the oven to 180°C/160°C fan/350°F/Gas 4.

Grease the base and sides of a 20cm (8in) square tin and line with baking parchment.

Melt the butter and chocolate together in the microwave in 30-second bursts, stirring in between each burst, until the chocolate is melted, then set aside.

Mix the eggs, vanilla and sugars together until just combined. Add the melted chocolate mixture to the eggs and sugar. Mix till smooth. Add the banana, flour and chocolate chips, if using, and mix until just combined.

Pour into the prepared tin and bake for 45–50 minutes. Remove from the oven when it still has a slight wobble in the middle and allow to cool completely in the tin. Remove from the tin and cut into 9 equal pieces.

Tip: If you want to add something different to your blondies, you can replace the white chocolate chips with dark chocolate or chopped nuts such as chopped almonds.

COCONUT TRAYBAKE

Prep Time 15–20 minutes
Cook Time 25–30 minutes
Serves 8
Type of banana: YELLOW
Dairy Free | Nut Free | Vegan

¼ tsp white wine vinegar
½ tsp baking powder
135g (4¾oz) caster sugar
120g (4¼oz) vegan margarine, softened
1½ tsps coconut oil, melted
2 bananas, mashed
1 tsp vanilla extract
150g (5¼oz) self-raising flour
40g (1½oz) desiccated coconut, plus extra to decorate

FOR THE ICING
150g (5¼oz) icing sugar
3 tbsps coconut milk

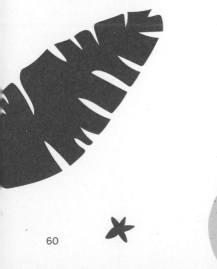

Preheat the oven to 180°C/160°C fan/350°F/Gas 4.

Grease the base and sides of a deep 20cm (8in) square tin and line with baking parchment.

Mix the vinegar and baking powder together in a bowl and then set aside.

In a separate bowl, beat the sugar and margarine together until pale and fluffy. Add the melted coconut oil, mashed banana, vanilla and the vinegar mixture to the sugar and margarine. Mix until mostly combined. Add the flour and desiccated coconut and mix until fully combined, but try not to overmix the batter.

Pour the batter into the prepared tin and bake for 25–30 minutes until a skewer comes out clean. Allow to cool completely in the tin.

To make the icing, sift the icing sugar into a bowl and add the coconut milk. Mix until smooth and then drizzle over the cooled cake. Sprinkle some extra coconut evenly over the top and, once the icing has set, cut into 8 pieces.

GOLDEN BANANA FLAPJACKS

Prep Time 10–15 minutes

Cook Time 15–20 minutes

Makes 9

Type of banana: YELLOW

Gluten Free | Nut Free

---

2 bananas
2 tbsps light brown sugar
3 tbsps golden syrup
70g (2½oz) sugar
150g (5¼oz) salted butter
400g (14oz) porridge oats

Preheat the oven to 200°C/180°C fan/400°F/Gas 6.

Line an 18cm (7in) square glass dish with baking parchment.

Slice the bananas lengthways and arrange them on the bottom of the glass dish. Evenly sprinkle the light brown sugar over the top of the bananas.

In a saucepan, melt the golden syrup, caster sugar and butter together over a low heat. Put the oats in a mixing bowl. Once the sugar has dissolved and the butter has melted, pour over the oats and mix thoroughly. Press the oat mixture into the dish on top of the bananas until the surface is flat and even.

Bake for 15–20 minutes or until lightly golden. Remove from the oven and allow to cool in the dish. Once cooled, turn out the flapjack onto a chopping board, banana side up, and carefully remove the baking parchment. Slice into 9 pieces and enjoy.

MUFFINS, BISCUITS AND TEA TIME TREATS

BANOFFEE CUPCAKES

Prep Time 30–35 minutes
Cook Time 15–20 minutes
Makes 12
Type of banana: BROWN
Nut Free

50g (1¾oz) salted butter, softened
20g (¾oz) cream cheese
175g (6oz) light brown sugar
2 bananas
2 eggs
½ tsp vanilla extract
200g (7oz) self-raising flour
½ tsp baking powder
½ tsp salt

FOR THE WHIPPED CREAM
300ml (1¼ cups) whipping cream
50g (1¾oz) icing sugar

FOR THE FILLING
4 tbsps ready-made toffee sauce

Preheat the oven to 180°C/160°C fan/350°F/Gas 4.

Line a 12-hole muffin tin with muffin cases.

Beat the butter, cream cheese and sugar together until pale and fluffy. In a separate bowl, mash the banana with the eggs and vanilla. Gradually beat this mixture into the butter and sugar. Sift the flour, baking powder and salt into the mixture and gently fold into the wet ingredients until fully incorporated.

Evenly distribute the mixture into the muffin cases, filling each case around three-quarters full. Bake for 15–20 minutes until the cupcakes are golden brown and spring back when gently pressed. Remove from the oven and leave in the tray to cool.

While the cupcakes are cooling,

make the whipped cream. Whisk the cream and sifted icing sugar together with an electric mixer on high speed to get soft-peak texture (be careful not to overwhip as the cream can separate).

When the cupcakes are cool, scoop a small hole in the centre of each cupcake with a melon baller or knife. Fill each hole with the toffee sauce, being careful not to fill higher than the surface of the cupcake.

Spoon a generous amount of the whipped cream on top of each cupcake.

FUN FACT

Bananas are grown in over 135 countries for their fruit and fibre. They are also used to create banana beer and banana wine, or simply grown as ornamental plants.

BREAKFAST BLUEBERRY MUFFINS

Prep Time 15–20 minutes
Cook Time 20–25 minutes
Makes 12
Type of banana: BROWN
Nut Free

70g (2½oz) salted butter, softened
170g (6oz) light brown sugar
2 bananas, mashed
1 tbsp maple syrup
2 eggs, beaten
200g (7oz) self-raising flour
1 tsp bicarbonate of soda
½ tsp salt
50g (1¾oz) porridge oats
40g (1½oz) blueberries

Preheat the oven to 180°C/160°C fan/350°F/Gas 4.

Line a 12-hole muffin tin with muffin cases.

Beat the butter and sugar together until pale and fluffy. Add the mashed banana, maple syrup and eggs and mix until just combined (the mixture may look a little odd at this point!).

Fold in the flour, bicarbonate of soda and salt until fully combined. Add the oats and blueberries. Mix until these are evenly distributed.

Divide the mixture equally between the muffin cases, filling each case around three-quarters full, and bake for 20–25 minutes until golden brown.

Allow to cool on a wire rack and then enjoy.

BANANA CUPCAKES

Prep Time 20–25 minutes
Cook Time 15–20 minutes
Makes 12
Type of banana: BROWN
Nut Free

60g (2oz) salted butter, softened
110g (4oz) caster sugar
1 egg, beaten
1 banana
2 tbsps plain yogurt
100g (3½oz) self-raising flour
½ tsp bicarbonate of soda
½ tsp baking powder

FOR THE FROSTING
125g (4½oz) mascarpone
100g (3½oz) cream cheese
100g (3½oz) icing sugar

Preheat the oven to 180°C/160°C fan/350°F/Gas 4.

Line a 12-hole muffin tin with muffin cases.

Beat the butter and sugar together until pale and fluffy. Beat the egg in gradually. Mash the banana and yogurt together in a separate bowl, then add this to the mixture.

Sift the flour, bicarbonate of soda and baking powder into the batter and gently fold until the dry ingredients are fully incorporated.

Evenly distribute the mixture into the muffin cases, filling each case around three-quarters full. Bake for 15–20 minutes until the cupcakes are golden brown. Remove from the oven and leave to cool on a wire rack.

While the cupcakes are cooling, sift the icing sugar and whisk with the mascarpone and cream cheese together with an electric mixer on high speed for 3 minutes until thick. When the cupcakes are cool, dollop a generous amount of frosting on top of each cupcake.

Tip: The yogurt in this recipe gives an extra lightness to the cupcakes.

BANANA, CARROT AND PECAN MUFFINS

Prep Time 15–20 minutes
Cook Time 20–25 minutes
Makes 12
Type of banana: BROWN

165g (5¾oz) caster sugar
1 tsp vanilla extract
70g (2½oz) salted butter, softened
2 eggs, beaten
2 bananas, mashed
75g (2¾oz) carrot, peeled and grated
200g (7oz) self-raising flour
1 tsp baking powder
¼ tsp salt
50g (1¾oz) pecan nuts, chopped

FOR THE GLAZE
½ tsp vanilla extract
50g (1¾oz) icing sugar
1 tbsp water

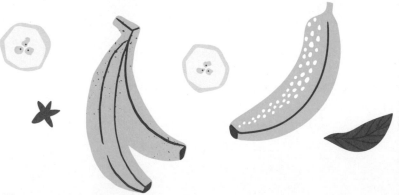

Preheat the oven to 180°C/160°C fan/350°F/Gas 4.

Line a 12-hole muffin tin with muffin cases.

Beat the sugar, vanilla and butter together until pale and fluffy. Gradually add the eggs, beating vigorously after each addition. Fold in the banana and carrot until evenly distributed. Fold in the flour, baking powder, salt and chopped pecans.

Divide the mixture evenly between the muffin cases, filling each case around three-quarters full, and then bake for 20–25 minutes or until they spring back when gently pressed. Remove from the oven. As soon as the muffins are out of the oven, make the glaze.

For the glaze, mix the vanilla, sifted icing sugar and water together until smooth.

Brush the glaze over the warm muffins and then allow to cool.

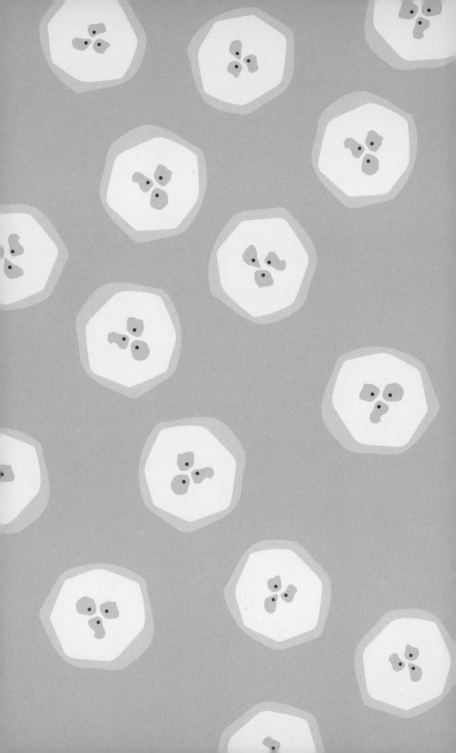

CHOCOLATE CHIP BANANA MUFFINS

Prep Time 10–15 minutes

Cook Time 20–25 minutes

Makes 12

Type of banana: YELLOW

Dairy Free | Vegan

300ml (1¼ cups) non-dairy milk
2 tsps vanilla extract
2 bananas, mashed
5 tbsps vegetable oil
240g (8½oz) caster sugar
250g (8¾oz) self-raising flour
½ tsp salt
60g (2oz) dark chocolate chips

Preheat the oven to 180°C/160°C fan/350°F/Gas 4.

Line a 12-hole muffin tin with muffin cases.

Mix all the ingredients, except the chocolate chips, together until smooth, then fold in the chocolate chips.

Divide the mixture evenly between the muffin cases and bake for 20–25 minutes until the muffins spring back when gently pressed and are slightly golden.

Allow to cool on a wire rack and enjoy for breakfast or whenever you crave them.

Tip: These muffins can be kept in the freezer for up to 1 month if you cannot eat them fast enough.

PEANUT BUTTER CUPCAKES

Prep Time 20–25 minutes
Cook Time 15–20 minutes
Makes 12
Type of banana: BROWN

60g (2oz) salted butter, softened
110g (4oz) caster sugar
1 egg, beaten
1 banana
2 tbsps cream cheese
100g (3½oz) self-raising flour
½ tsp bicarbonate of soda
½ tsp baking powder

FOR THE ICING
150g (5¼oz) smooth peanut butter
50g (1¾oz) cream cheese
150g (5¼oz) icing sugar
1 tbsp semi-skimmed milk

Preheat the oven to 170°C/150°C fan/325°F/Gas 3.

Line a 12-hole muffin tin with muffin cases.

Beat the butter and sugar together until pale and fluffy. Beat in the egg. Mash the banana and cream cheese together in a separate bowl, then stir this into the butter mixture.

Sift the flour, bicarbonate of soda and baking powder into the batter and fold it in.

Pour the mixture into the muffin cases, filling each case around three-quarters full.

Bake for 15–20 minutes until the cupcakes are golden brown and a skewer comes out clean when poked into the centre of a cupcake. Remove from the oven and leave to cool on a wire rack.

For the icing, whisk the peanut butter, cream cheese and sifted icing sugar together until smooth. Add the milk and then whisk for a further 2 minutes until it is fluffy.

Dollop a generous helping of icing on top of each cooled cupcake and enjoy.

Tip: The banana gives the cupcakes a soft texture without a strong banana flavour.

BANANA NUT COOKIES

Prep Time 20–25 minutes + 30 minutes chilling
Cook Time 10–12 minutes
Makes 8–10
Type of banana: BROWN

60g (2oz) butter, softened
60g (2oz) light brown sugar
60g (2oz) caster sugar
1 small banana, mashed
1 tsp vanilla extract
110g (4oz) self-raising flour
¼ tsp salt
60g (2oz) pecan nuts, chopped
30g (1oz) hazelnuts, chopped

Line two large baking trays with baking parchment.

Beat the butter and sugars together with an electric mixer on high speed for about 2 minutes until fluffy.

Add the mashed banana, vanilla, flour and salt and mix until just combined. Fold in the chopped nuts.

Place the mixture in the fridge for about 30 minutes or until firm.

Preheat the oven to 220°C/200°C fan/425°F/Gas 7.

Remove the mix from the fridge and roll into 8–10 equal balls (around 1½ tablespoons of mixture for each ball). Place them evenly on the baking trays, making sure that each ball has enough space to expand in the oven, and then bake for 10–12 minutes until each cookie has a golden edge and has flattened out.

Remove from the oven and allow the cookies to cool completely on the baking trays. The cookies will set as they cool down.

FUN FACT

Other than the most
common yellow variety,
bananas can also be
green, red or purple.

CHOCOLATE CHIP SCO-KIES

Prep Time 20–25 minutes + 30 minutes chilling
Cook Time 12 minutes
Makes 16
Type of banana: BROWN
Dairy Free | Vegan

Sco-kies: a delicious mix between a scone and a cookie!

1 banana, mashed
250g (8¾oz) caster sugar
50g (1¾oz) cold-pressed coconut oil
3 tbsps dairy-free milk
2 tsps vanilla extract
100g (3½oz) vegan chocolate chips (milk or white chocolate)
300g (10½oz) plain flour
½ tsp baking powder
¼ tsp bicarbonate of soda

Line two baking trays with baking parchment.

Mix the banana, sugar and cold coconut oil together until smooth. Mix in the milk and vanilla and then add the chocolate chips.

Sift in the dry ingredients and mix until fully incorporated. Place the mixture in the fridge around 30 minutes or until the mixture is firm (this will make it easier to divide into balls).

Preheat the oven to 200°C/180°C fan/400°F/Gas 6.

Divide the mixture into 16 even balls and place them on the prepared baking trays, giving plenty of space for each ball to spread in the oven.

Bake for 12 minutes until slightly golden, turning the trays around halfway through the time. Once baked, allow to cool on the baking trays and then enjoy!

Tip: You can freeze the balls of dough and bake them from frozen. Just add an extra 5 minutes to the cooking time.

COCONUT BISCUITS

Prep Time 10–15 minutes + 1 hour chilling
Cook Time 10–12 minutes
Makes 20
Type of banana: YELLOW
Dairy Free | Vegan

50g (1¾oz) icing sugar
1 tsp vanilla extract
100g (3½oz) vegan margarine, softened
150g (5¼oz) plain flour
1 tsp coconut oil
65g (2¼oz) ground almonds
1 small banana, blended
Handful of desiccated coconut

Line two large baking trays with baking parchment.

Mix together the icing sugar, vanilla, margarine, flour and coconut oil until you have a dry dough.

Add the ground almonds and banana and knead by hand until you have a firm ball of dough. Turn the dough out onto the work surface and roll to about 1.5cm (½in) thick. Using a 6cm (2in) diameter biscuit cutter, cut out as many biscuits as you can. Bring the leftover dough together and roll out again until you run out of dough. Place all the biscuits on the prepared baking trays, leaving at least 2cm (¾in) between each biscuit.

Sprinkle a little bit of the desiccated coconut onto each biscuit and then gently press it into the biscuits. Chill the biscuits in the fridge for 1 hour until they have set.

Before removing the biscuits from the fridge, preheat the oven to 200°C/180°C fan/400°F/ Gas 6. Once the oven is hot, bake the biscuits straight from the fridge for 10–12 minutes, turning the tray around halfway through the time, until slightly golden around the edge. Allow to cool on the baking trays.

ÉCLAIRS WITH BANANA CREAM FILLING

Prep Time 40–50 minutes

Cook Time 30–40 minutes

Makes 12

Type of banana: YELLOW

Nut Free

FOR THE CHOUX PASTRY
45g (1½oz) salted butter, cut into small cubes
115ml (4 fl oz) water
50g (1¾oz) plain flour, sifted
2 eggs, beaten

FOR THE BANANA CREAM
50g (1¾oz) white chocolate
125ml (½ cup) whipping cream
1 large banana, mashed

TO DECORATE
50g (1¾oz) white chocolate
Dark chocolate, for grating

Preheat the oven to 200°C/180°C fan/400°F/Gas 6.

Line two baking trays with baking parchment. Using a ruler, mark 12 lines around 8cm (3½in) long on each piece of parchment, leaving plenty of space between each line, and then flip the parchment over.

Prepare a piping bag with a large round piping nozzle around 1.5cm (½in) wide.

For the choux pastry, place the butter and water in a saucepan and heat gently. Once the butter has melted, turn up the heat and bring the mixture to a fast boil.

Once boiling, remove from the heat and add the sifted flour. Vigorously beat the mixture with a wooden spoon for around 30 seconds and then return to the heat. Keep beating the pastry until it starts to pull away from the sides of the pan and is lump free. Remove the pan from the heat and allow it to cool.

Add the beaten egg a little at a time, making sure to beat the mixture thoroughly after each addition. Keep adding the egg until the mixture is smooth and glossy but still has a pipeable consistency (you may not need to use all the egg. You might also find that you need a little more liquid; if so, just add water a few drops at a time).

Fill the piping bag with the pastry and remove the baking parchment from the baking trays. Pipe a little of the mixture on your baking trays to allow the parchment to stick to the trays. Replace the baking parchment on the trays and evenly pipe the batter onto them, using the lines you marked as your guide.

Bake for 30–40 minutes, turning the trays around for the final 10 minutes. The choux pastry should have puffed up, have a golden colour and sound hollow when tapped. Once baked, leave on the baking tray to cool completely. When cooled, carefully make two small holes on the bottom of each éclair for the piping tip.

Continued overleaf

To make the banana cream, place the white chocolate, cream and mashed banana in a heatproof bowl. Place the bowl on top of a pan of simmering water, making sure that the bowl doesn't touch the water. Occasionally whisk the mixture so the chocolate doesn't burn. Once the chocolate has fully melted, remove the bowl from the heat and then, using a hand blender, blend the cream until smooth. Allow to cool to room temperature and then whisk the cream to stiff peaks.

Fill a piping bag with the banana cream and then cut a small hole at the end. Pipe the banana cream into the holes you created on the bases of the éclairs.

For the decoration, melt the white chocolate in the microwave in 20 second bursts, stirring after each burst. Carefully dip the top of each éclair into the chocolate and then grate some dark chocolate over the top. Enjoy!

Tip: The unfilled éclairs can be kept for a couple of days in an airtight container but once you fill them, they are better eaten on the same day.

BANANA CREAM DOUGHNUTS

Prep Time 30 minutes + 2–3 hours proving
Cook Time 20–25 minutes
Makes 12–14
Type of banana: YELLOW
Nut Free

FOR THE DOUGHNUTS
5 tbsps full-fat milk, lukewarm
5g (¼oz) instant yeast
25g (1oz) caster sugar
250g (8¾oz) strong white flour
1 tsp salt
2 eggs
130g (4½oz) unsalted butter, softened
Vegetable oil, for frying

FOR THE BANANA CREAM
100g (3½oz) white chocolate
250ml (1 cup) whipping cream
1 large banana, mashed
Icing sugar, for dusting

Stir together the warm milk, instant yeast and 1 teaspoon of the sugar and leave for 5–10 minutes until it has doubled in size.

Mix the flour, salt, eggs, butter, remaining sugar and the yeast mix in a mixer until a tacky dough is formed (around 10–15 minutes). It is best to use a hook attachment at this stage (see Tip).

Form a ball with the dough and place into a buttered bowl to prevent it from sticking. Cover the bowl with a damp tea towel and leave in a warm place for 1½–2 hours until it has doubled in size.

Turn out the dough onto a greased surface and roll it to 1.5cm (½in) thickness. Cut out rounds with a 6cm (2in) round cookie cutter and place on a baking tray lined with baking parchment. Keep rerolling and cutting out as many doughnut discs as you can until all dough is used. Cover the doughnuts with a clean tea towel and allow to rise for 45 minutes–1 hour or until doubled in size.

Half fill a heavy saucepan with oil and heat to 180°C (350°F). Fry the doughnuts by dropping several of them at a time into the oil and allow to become golden before turning over (around 1–2 minutes per side). Make sure the oil doesn't get too cold at this stage as this can make the doughnuts very oily. Transfer the doughnuts to sheets of paper towel and allow to cool.

To make the banana cream, place the white chocolate, cream and mashed banana in a heatproof bowl. Place the bowl on top of a pan of simmering water, making sure that the bowl doesn't touch the water. Whisk the mixture occasionally so the chocolate doesn't burn. Once the chocolate has fully melted, remove the bowl from the heat and then, using a hand blender, blend the cream until smooth. Allow to cool to room temperature and then whisk the cream to stiff peaks.

Place the banana cream in a piping bag with a large, round metal tip. Poke a hole on one side of the cooled doughnuts. Place the tip of the piping bag into the hole and fill each doughnut with banana cream.

Sift a generous helping of icing sugar over the top to serve.

Tip: This recipe is easier done in a stand mixer but if you do not have one you can use the hook attachment of an electric mixer. Fresh doughnuts are the best doughnuts. That sentiment is true with this recipe as these doughnuts are best eaten on the day they are made.

BANANA PENGUIN LOLLIES

Prep Time 10–15 minutes + 15 minutes freezing

Makes 8

Type of banana: YELLOW

Gluten Free | Nut Free

---

4 bananas
8 dried apricots
100g (3½oz) dark chocolate
16 mini marshmallows

Cut the bananas in half, creating 8 equal-sized pieces.

To prepare the apricots, carefully cut a triangle out of each, with the point of the triangle starting from the middle of the apricot. The 8 triangles will be the beaks and the 8 remaining pieces of apricot will be the feet. Set aside.

Slide a lolly stick into the flat base of each banana piece, place on a tray lined with baking parchment and place in the freezer for 10 minutes.

While the bananas are in the freezer, place the chocolate in a glass bowl and then place the bowl over a pan of simmering water, making sure the water doesn't touch the base of the bowl. Once the chocolate has melted, remove from the heat and take the bananas out of the freezer.

Holding onto the lolly stick, dip each banana into the chocolate, covering the top and what will be the back of the penguin. If you are having trouble dipping the bananas into the chocolate or if the amount of chocolate is getting too shallow, you can transfer the chocolate to a tall mug to make it easier.

Use some of the chocolate to place 2 little dots in the centre of each marshmallow to create the eyes.

Use the remaining chocolate to stick apricot triangle beaks and feet onto the penguins and then return them to the freezer for 5 minutes to fully set.

Tips: This is a fun recipe to get the kids involved. To make it suitable for vegans you can buy vegan marshmallows from certain stores.

FUN FACT

Bananas are one of the most wasted
foods because they are thrown away
when they get too ripe to eat, but
there are many ways to use up these
ripe bananas.

BANANA GHOST LOLLIES

Prep Time 10–15 minutes + 15 minutes freezing

Makes 8

Type of banana: YELLOW

Gluten Free | Nut Free

---

4 bananas
140g (5oz) white chocolate
30g (1oz) dark chocolate

Cut the bananas in half, creating 8 equal-sized pieces. Slide a lolly stick into the flat base of each banana piece, place on a tray lined with baking parchment and place in the freezer for 10 minutes.

While the bananas are in the freezer, place the white chocolate in a glass bowl and then place the bowl over a pan of simmering water, making sure the water doesn't touch the base of the bowl). Once the chocolate has melted, remove from the heat and take the bananas out of the freezer.

Holding onto the lolly stick, dip each banana into the chocolate, fully covering each piece. Place the bananas back on the tray and then into the fridge.

Melt the dark chocolate in a glass bowl over simmering water, making sure the bowl doesn't touch the water. Once melted remove from the heat, and take the bananas out of the fridge.

Using the dark chocolate and a teaspoon, draw ghoulish eyes and a mouth on each banana. It doesn't need to be neat as it will add to the ghostly effect.

Place the bananas back in the fridge for 5 minutes till fully set.

Tip: To make this recipe suitable for vegans you can purchase vegan white chocolate from certain shops.

CANDIED BANANA PEEL

Prep Time 5 minutes + overnight drying
Cook Time 40 minutes
Makes About 100 candies
Type of banana: YELLOW
Dairy Free | Gluten Free | Nut Free | Vegan

---

3 bananas
200g (7oz) granulated sugar
200ml (7 fl oz) water
Caster sugar, for coating

Thoroughly wash the bananas to remove any bitter residue or pesticides from the peel. Remove the peel from each bananas in three long strands.

Cut off the ends and then scrape off the white inside of the peel with a spoon. Cut each length in half and then into long, thin strands.

Bring a pan of water to the boil and add the banana peel. Boil for 20 minutes and then drain. If the water starts to become very brown, throw away the water, bring a fresh pan of water to the boil and continue cooking.

In a separate pan, bring the sugar and measured water up to a simmer. Add the peel and gently boil for 20 minutes.

Drain the peel and lay on a wire rack. Sprinkle the peel with caster sugar and allow it to dry out overnight.

Tips: Use as a decoration for other bakes or wrap in gift bags for someone special. You can also use the peel in the Candied Banana Chocolate Bars recipe on the opposite page.

CANDIED BANANA CHOCOLATE BARS

Prep Time 15–20 minutes + 10 minutes chilling

Cook Time 5–10 minutes

Serves 8

Type of banana: YELLOW

Dairy Free | Gluten Free | Vegan

200g (7oz) dark chocolate
50g (1¾oz) Candied Banana Peel (see opposite page)
Handful of pistachios, chopped
Handful of desiccated coconut

Line a 20 x 10cm (8 x 4in) baking tray with baking parchment.

Half fill a saucepan with water and bring it up to a simmer over a low heat.

Place the chocolate in a heatproof bowl and place this over the simmering water. You don't want the bowl to touch the water so you may need to use quite a large bowl.

Stir the chocolate occasionally and when it is fully melted, remove it from the heat. Dry the outside of the bowl to make sure you don't get any water In your chocolate later on.

Pour the chocolate on to the prepared baking tray. Spread the chocolate until it is, mostly, flat and even. Before the chocolate sets, randomly distribute the Candied Banana Peel, chopped pistachios and coconut over the top.

Place the chocolate in the fridge for 10 minutes to set. Once set, you can break the chocolate into individual shards.

Tip: A couple of shards in a cellophane bag can be a great gift or you can just keep it all for yourself as a treat.

SWEET TATALE (PLANTAIN PANCAKES)

Prep Time 10 minutes + 25 minutes resting

Cook Time 15–20 minutes

Makes 4–5

Type of banana: BLACK PLANTAIN

Nut Free

---

2 very ripe/black plantains
1½ tsps grated fresh root ginger
¼ tsp ground cinnamon
1 tbsp honey
¼ tsp salt
70g (2½oz) plain flour
Vegetable oil, for frying

TO SERVE (OPTIONAL)
Ice cream
Golden syrup

In a bowl, mash the plantain until mostly smooth (you can use a hand blender to help). Stir in the grated ginger, cinnamon, honey and salt.

Add the flour and stir until fully combined and then allow the mixture to rest for around 25 minutes.

After resting, heat a shallow layer of oil in a non-stick frying pan over a medium heat. Add around 2 tablespoons of mixture to the pan and then flatten this slightly to make a round patty. Fry each patty for around 2 minutes on each side or until it is a dark golden colour. Repeat until all of the mixture has been used.

Enjoy as a snack or as a dessert with ice cream and golden syrup.

Tip: Tatale is pronounced ta-ta-lay. Use very, very ripe plantains with skins that are almost completely black.

DESSERTS AND
PUDDINGS

CARAMELIZED BANANA WAFFLES

Prep Time 10–15 minutes + 15 minutes resting
Cook Time 15 minutes
Serves 4
Type of banana: YELLOW
Nut Free

200g (7oz) self-raising flour
½ tsp baking powder
¼ tsp salt
2 tbsps caster sugar
½ tsp ground cinnamon
2 eggs
250ml (1 cup) semi-skimmed milk
1 banana, mashed
100g (3½oz) salted butter, melted
Ice cream, to serve

FOR THE CARAMELIZED BANANAS
75g (2¾oz) light muscovado sugar
50g (1¾oz) butter
1 tbsp maple syrup
2 bananas, sliced

Whisk the flour, baking powder, salt, sugar and cinnamon together. In a separate bowl, mix together the eggs, milk, banana and melted butter until combined.

Add the wet ingredients to the dry ingredients and whisk until there are no lumps left. Leave the batter to rest for 15 minutes.

Grease a waffle iron and heat according to the manufacturer's instructions. Pour in the batter and cook until golden (around 3 minutes). Repeat until all the batter has been used, which should make around 4 waffles.

To make the caramelized bananas, heat the sugar and butter in a saucepan over a medium–low heat, whisking continuously to make sure it doesn't burn on the bottom. Bring to the boil for 15 seconds. Remove from the heat and whisk in the maple syrup. Fold in the sliced bananas until each slice has an even coating of syrup.

Serve the waffles with a generous amount of caramelized banana and a scoop of ice cream.

BANANA PANCAKES

Prep Time 5–10 minutes
Cook Time 20–25 minutes
Makes 10 small pancakes
Type of banana: BROWN
Nut Free

150g (5¼oz) self-raising flour
1 egg
100ml (3 ½ fl oz) semi-skimmed milk
1 banana, mashed
Vegetable oil, for frying

TO SERVE (OPTIONAL)
Golden syrup
Ice cream

Whisk together the flour, egg and milk until smooth with no lumps of flour. Add the banana and blend together using a stick blender.

Add 1 tablespoon of oil to a non-stick frying pan and heat over a medium heat.

Pour about 3 tablespoons of batter into the frying pan and cook for about 1 minute, until the bottom is golden brown and the top appears 'dry'. Flip and cook the other side for 1 minute.

Remove from the pan and keep warm. Add more oil to the pan as needed and repeat until all the batter has been used.

Serve with golden syrup and your favourite ice cream, if you like.

FUN FACT

Banana flour has even been invented and was historically used in Jamaica and parts of Africa as a cheaper alternative to standard flour.

BANANA FRITTERS

Prep Time 15 minutes + 1 hour resting (optional)
Cook Time 15 minutes
Makes 10–12
Type of banana: BROWN
Nut Free

100g (3½oz) self-raising flour
½ tsp bicarbonate of soda
¼ tsp ground cinnamon
1 egg
135ml (4½ fl oz) semi-skimmed milk
3 bananas
Vegetable oil, for frying

TO SERVE
Runny honey or golden syrup
Ice cream

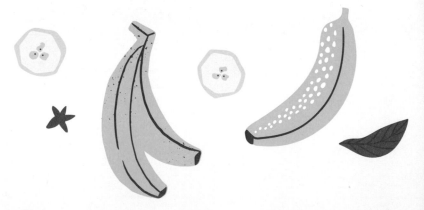

Whisk together the flour, bicarbonate of soda, cinnamon, egg and milk until smooth. If you have time, allow the batter to rest for 1 hour.

Slice the bananas diagonally and dip into the batter, making sure that each slice gets an even coating of batter.

Half fill a large saucepan with oil and heat it up to 180°C (350°F). Carefully place a maximum of 5 banana slices into the oil one at a time so that the temperature of the oil doesn't reduce.

Remove from the oil after 3–4 minutes or once they have turned a golden brown colour all over, and place on paper towels to absorb any excess oil. Repeat with all the slices, cooking a maximum of 5 at a time.

Serve warm with honey or golden syrup and a scoop of your favourite ice cream.

Tip: Once you are comfortable making banana fritters, why not try other fruit? Apples work well with this recipe too.

BANANA SUZETTES

Prep Time 5 minutes
Cook Time 5–10 minutes
Serves 4
Type of banana: YELLOW
Gluten Free | Nut Free

50g (1¾oz) unsalted butter
4 bananas, sliced diagonally
3 tbsps demerara sugar
Zest and juice of 1 orange
2 tbsps brandy or rum
Ice cream, to serve

Melt the butter in a large frying pan and sauté the bananas over a medium–high heat for 2–3 minute or until golden.

Turn the heat down to low and evenly sprinkle the sugar over the top of the bananas. Add the orange zest and juice and cook for a further 1 minute.

Add the brandy or rum and carefully ignite it. The flame will reduce as the alcohol burns away.

Once all the alcohol has been burnt off, remove the pan from the heat and then serve the bananas with ice cream, pouring any of the remaining sauce in the pan over the top of the ice cream.

Tip: Once you are comfortable with this recipe you can try it with other fruit or liqueurs, for example, orange segments and cognac work great together.

BBQ BANANA

Prep Time 5 minutes
Cook Time 15 minutes
Serves 4
Type of banana: YELLOW
Gluten Free

---

4 bananas
60g (2oz) chocolate (choose your favourite), roughly chopped

TO SERVE
Ice cream
Chopped nuts

If using a gas barbecue (grill), preheat the barbecue on a low heat with a closed lid. If using a charcoal barbecue, light the barbecue and wait until the charcoal is hot and has turned ashy.

Peel the bananas and place each on a sheet of foil. Make sure the foil is large enough to fully wrap the banana. Make a thin slice down the middle of each of the bananas. Portion the chocolate between the bananas, pushing it gently into the slits.

Wrap the bananas in the foil, then place them directly on the barbecue and cook for 15 minutes, turning them occasionally.

Carefully remove from the barbecue and take off the foil. Place the bananas on a serving dish and serve with your favourite ice cream and chopped nuts.

Tip: If you are using a gas barbecue with a lid, you can put the bananas on the barbecue once it has been switched off. Just place the bananas on the grill rack and close the lid; they will cook in the residual heat and you can come back to them when you're ready.

BANANA UPSIDE DOWN CAKE

Prep Time 15–20 minutes

Cook Time 40–45 minutes

Serves 9

Type of banana: YELLOW

Nut Free

---

2 bananas
15g (½oz) light muscovado sugar
150g (5¼oz) salted butter, softened
50g (1¾oz) crème fraîche
1 tsp vanilla extract
200g (7oz) caster sugar
4 eggs
200g (7oz) self-raising flour
Custard or ice cream, to serve

Preheat the oven to 180°C/160°C fan/350°F/Gas 4.

Grease the base and sides of a 23 x 18cm (9 x 7in) baking tin and line with baking parchment.

Slice the bananas lengthways and place them side down on the prepared baking tray – you should be able to fit all four slices next to each other along the base of the tin. Sprinkle the muscovado sugar evenly over the top of the bananas.

Beat together the butter, crème fraîche, vanilla and caster sugar until pale and fluffy.

Beat in 2 of the eggs until just combined then add half of the flour until just mixed. Add the remaining 2 eggs and remaining flour and mix until fully combined.

Spoon the mixture on top of the bananas and bake for 40–45 minutes until springy to the touch.

Leave to cool in the tray for 10 minutes then turn it onto a cooling rack. Cut into 9 squares and serve warm with custard or ice cream.

Tip: This pudding is best eaten the same day, still warm.

FUN FACT

There are different ideas regarding the origin of the name of the banana. One idea is that it originated from the Arabic word 'banan', which means finger.

BANANA NUT SUNDAE

Prep Time 15 minutes

Cook Time 5–10 minutes

Serves 4

Type of banana: YELLOW

Gluten Free

---

4 bananas, sliced
500g (1lb) ice cream (choose your favourite)
100g (3½oz) nuts, chopped (choose your favourite)

FOR THE FUDGE SAUCE
50g (1¾oz) salted butter
100g (3½oz) light brown sugar
2 tbsps maple syrup
100ml (3½ fl oz) double cream

To make the fudge sauce, bring the butter, light brown sugar and maple syrup to the boil in a pan over a low heat, stirring continuously so that it doesn't catch on the bottom. Once brought to the boil, remove from the heat and gradually whisk in the cream (it may spit, so be careful). Set aside to cool.

Layer the bananas, ice cream, nuts and fudge sauce in sundae glasses or bowls, topping with the last of the fudge sauce and a sprinkle of chopped nuts.

BANANA PRALINE PARFAIT

Prep Time 30–35 minutes + overnight freezing

Cook Time 5 minutes

Serves 8–10

Type of banana: YELLOW

Gluten Free

FOR THE PRALINE
120g (4¼oz) caster sugar
3 tbsps water
100g (3½oz) whole blanched hazelnuts

FOR THE PARFAIT
4 bananas, 2 mashed and 2 sliced, to serve
2 tsps lemon juice
300ml (1¼ cups) double cream
2 egg whites
100g (3½oz) caster sugar

Line a large baking tray with baking parchment and grease a 1kg (2lb) loaf tin and line with baking parchment.

To make the praline, place the sugar and water in a saucepan and place over a low heat until the sugar has completely dissolved. Increase to a medium heat and bring to the boil for around 3 minutes. Stir in the hazelnuts – at this point the sugar will crystallize, but there is no need to panic! The sugar around the bottom of the pan will caramelize so it is important to stir occasionally to make sure it doesn't burn. Eventually you will get hazelnuts that are evenly coated in caramel. Tip the nuts on to the prepared baking tray, spread evenly, then leave to cool.

Once cooled, break into pieces and then crush the nuts to a large breadcrumb texture in a food processor.

In a small bowl, mix the mashed banana and half the lemon juice together and set aside. In another bowl, whip the cream to soft peaks and set aside. In a glass bowl, whip the egg whites and remaining lemon juice until it turns white and frothy. Keep whisking while gradually adding the sugar until you get stiff peaks and a shiny meringue.

Fold the cream, banana mix and praline crumbs (leaving around 50g/1¾oz of praline aside for serving) into the meringue. Spoon the mixture into the prepared loaf tin and smooth the top.

Place in the freezer until firm, ideally overnight.

To serve, place the parfait in the fridge for 10 minutes to soften slightly. Demould the parfait from the loaf tin and cut into slices. Serve with a sprinkle of the leftover praline and the sliced bananas.

Tip: This parfait can be stored in the freezer for 2 months.

TROPICAL FRUIT PUDDING

Prep Time 30–35 minutes + 6 hours chilling
Cook Time 5 minutes
Serves 8–10
Type of banana: YELLOW
Nut Free

400g (14oz) peeled mango (the equivalent of 1 large mango)
2 bananas
150g (5¼oz) peeled blood orange (the equivalent of 1 large orange)
3 tbsps water
70g (2½oz) caster sugar
Zest and juice of 1 lime
7 slices day-old medium-cut white bread

TO SERVE
Cream
Fresh fruit

Line a 500ml (2 cup) bowl with clingfilm, overlapping the clingfilm layers if required. Allow the clingfilm to overhang on all sides by about 10cm (4in).

Chop all the fruit into small cubes. Put the blood orange in a bowl and set aside.

Place the sugar and water in a large pan and place over a low heat until the sugar dissolves. Bring to the boil for around 1 minute and then add the mango, banana and lime zest. Cook for 2 minutes over a low heat, stirring occasionally to make sure the fruit isn't sticking to the bottom (try not to stir too often because you don't want to break it up too much). When ready, the fruit should be mostly intact and softer, surrounded by a pale orange juice.

Sieve the juice into a bowl and set the fruit aside to cool.

While the fruit and juice are cooling, cut the crusts off the slices of bread. Cut 4 slices in half at a slight angle to create 8 wonky rectangles. Cut 1 slice into 4 triangles. Leave 2 slices whole.

Dip one of the whole slices into the fruit juice for a few seconds just to coat it. Press this into the bottom of the lined bowl. Repeat with the rectangular pieces, placing them around the sides of the bowl so that they fit tightly together. If you need to trim some slices to make them fit that's fine.

Spoon the cooked fruit into the centre, dotting blood orange among it. Finally, dip the remaining whole slice of bread into the juice and place on top of the fruit and fill in any gaps with the dipped triangles if needed.

Trim off any overhang of bread and then seal over with the overhang of clingfilm. Place a side plate over the top and use some tins to weight it down.

Refrigerate for at least 6 hours and ideally overnight. Once chilled, turn upside down onto a serving plate. Serve with lots of cream and your favourite fresh berries.

DRUNKEN CHOCOLATE PUDDING

Prep Time 35–40 minutes
Cook Time 50 minutes
Serves 6–8
Type of banana: BROWN
Gluten Free

140g (5oz) dates, pitted and chopped
4 tbsps Marsala wine or sherry
1 banana
100g (3½oz) salted butter
140g (5oz) dark chocolate, chopped
3 eggs
100g (3½oz) caster sugar
50g (1¾oz) light brown sugar
1 tsp vanilla extract
115g (4oz) ground almonds
2 tbsps cocoa powder, plus extra to decorate
Cream or custard, to serve

Preheat the oven to 180°C/160°C fan/350°F/Gas 4.

Thoroughly grease a 1.25 litre (2 pint) pudding basin.

Gently heat the dates and Marsala or sherry in a pan until hot but not boiling. Remove from the heat and leave to cool until the dates have absorbed most of the liquid. Blend the dates with any remaining liquid until smooth using a stick blender. Add the banana and blend again.

Melt the butter and chocolate in the microwave, stirring at 30-second intervals until fully melted. Stir into the date mixture and set aside. Separate 2 of the eggs.

Whisk the sugars, 1 egg and the 2 egg yolks until they have doubled in volume and are paler. Fold in the chocolate and date mixture.

Add the vanilla and sift in the ground almonds and cocoa powder. Fold the mixture until everything is combined.

In a separate bowl, whisk the egg whites until you get stiff peaks. Gently fold this into the chocolate batter in stages and then gently pour into the prepared bowl. Bake for 50 minutes until a crust has formed.

Remove from the oven and cool in the pudding basin for 15 minutes (it will sink and crack as it cools). Once it has cooled slightly, carefully turn the pudding out onto a serving plate and sprinkle with cocoa powder before serving with cream or custard.

BANANA CREAM PIE

Prep Time 30–40 minutes + 1 hour and 20 minutes cooling

Cook Time 25 minutes

Serves 8–10

Type of banana: YELLOW

Nut Free

FOR THE PASTRY
60g (2oz) caster sugar
1 egg white
120g (4¼oz) salted butter
180g (6¼oz) plain flour, plus extra for dusting

FOR THE FILLING
370ml (1½ cups) full-fat milk
150ml (5 fl oz) double cream
100g (3½oz) granulated sugar
Pinch of salt
4 egg yolks
30g (1oz) cornflour
2 tsp vanilla extract
30g (1oz) unsalted butter, softened
3 bananas

FOR THE CREAM
200ml (¾ cup) double cream
30g (1oz) icing sugar
Cocoa powder, to decorate (optional)

To make the pastry, mix together the sugar and egg white in a large bowl until the sugar has dissolved. Add the butter and flour and knead until it forms a smooth dough. Flatten the dough slightly and then wrap in clingfilm. Place the dough in the fridge for around 45 minutes.

Remove the dough from the fridge and roll out on a well-floured work surface to around 1cm (½in) thickness. Line a deep, round 20cm (8in) tin with the pastry, letting any excess hang over the edge of the tin. Place this in the fridge for 10 minutes.

Preheat the oven to 200°C/180°C fan/400°F/Gas 6. Remove the pastry case from the fridge, line the inside with baking parchment and fill to the top with baking beads.

Blind bake the pastry for 20 minutes until the pastry holds its shape. Remove the beads and

baking parchment and bake for a further 5 minutes to give the pastry some colour. Remove from the oven and trim off any excess pastry while it is still hot and then set aside to cool (you can save any of the trimmings for decoration).

Meanwhile, for the filling, add the milk, cream, sugar and salt to a saucepan over a medium heat. Whisk the ingredients until the sugar has dissolved. Bring the mix to a simmer, whisking occasionally to stop it from burning. Once the milk mix starts to simmer, remove from the heat.

In a heatproof bowl, whisk together the egg yolks, cornflour and vanilla until smooth. Slowly pour around 100ml (3½ fl oz) of the milk mix into the eggs while continually whisking. Once fully combined, slowly pour the egg mix back into the pan while

Continued overleaf

continually whisking again (this stage is to stop the eggs from scrambling).

Place the pan back over the heat and cook for around 2 minutes until thick and large bubbles rise to the top when it's boiling, making sure to whisk the mixture while cooking.

Pour the custard into a heatproof dish and whisk in the butter. Place clingfilm directly on top of the custard to stop a skin from forming. Allow to cool for around 25 minutes.

While the custard is cooling, slice the bananas and place them evenly over the cooled pastry base (save a few slices for decoration). When the filling is cool but not cold, spread it on top of the bananas. Place in the fridge for 10 minutes to fully set.

While the custard is setting, whisk the cream and sifted icing sugar together to stiff peaks, making sure not to overwhisk. Dollop the cream onto the centre of the cooled custard, creating random peaks of cream. If you have saved any of the pastry trimmings, you can sprinkle these around the edge of the pie and then decorate the top of the cream with the remaining slices of banana and a sprinkling of cocoa powder, if you like.

The original wild bananas were a lot smaller than the common variety sold today – about the length of a finger.

BANOFFEE PIE

Prep Time 35–40 minutes + 20 minutes cooling
Cook Time 10 minutes
Serves 8–10
Type of banana: YELLOW
Nut Free

FOR THE BASE
150g (5¼oz) digestive biscuits
80g (2¾oz) salted butter, melted

FOR THE TOFFEE FILLING
75g (2¾oz) butter
75g (2¾oz) light brown sugar
1 x 397g (14oz) tin sweetened condensed milk
1 tsp vanilla extract
4 tbsps double cream
2 bananas

FOR THE TOPPING
300ml (1¼ cups) double cream
50g (1¾oz) icing sugar

Grease the base and sides of a 20cm (8in) springform tin.

For the base, place the biscuits in a food processor and blend until the biscuits have been broken down into an even crumb texture. Mix together the crushed biscuits and melted butter. Press this mixture into the base of the pie tin and chill for 10 minutes.

Meanwhile, for the filling, place the butter, sugar, condensed milk and vanilla in a saucepan and cook over a medium heat. Whisk continuously, making sure the bottom doesn't burn. Bring to the boil and then reduce the heat, continuously whisking. Cook until dark golden brown and then pour into a heatproof bowl. Whisk in the cream and set aside to cool.

Slice the bananas and place them evenly over the chilled base. When the toffee is cool but not cold, spread it on top of the bananas.

For the topping, whisk the cream and sifted icing sugar together to stiff peaks, making sure not to overwhisk.

Dollop the cream all over the top of the toffee, creating random peaks of cream.

Tip: You can replace the digestive biscuits in the base with your favourite biscuit, such as ginger nuts or chocolate digestives.

SELF-SAUCING CHOCOLATE PUDDING

Prep Time 15–20 minutes

Cook Time 30–35 minutes

Serves 9–10

Type of banana: BROWN

Nut Free

250g (8¾oz) self-raising flour
140g (5oz) caster sugar
50g (1¾oz) cocoa powder
1 tsp baking powder
Pinch of salt
2 eggs, beaten
4 tbsps Irish cream liqueur (optional)
2 bananas, mashed
50ml (2 fl oz) semi-skimmed milk
100g (3½oz) salted butter
Icing sugar, for dusting
Cream, to serve

FOR THE SAUCE
250ml (1 cup) boiling water
100g (3½oz) light brown sugar
2 tbsps cocoa powder
4 tbsps Irish cream liqueur

Preheat the oven to 180°C/160°C fan/ 350°F/Gas 4.

Grease the base of a deep 20cm (8in) square dish and line with baking parchment.

Mix together the flour, sugar, cocoa, baking powder and salt. Add the eggs, Irish cream liqueur, if using, and mashed banana to the dry ingredients and mix until mostly combined

Heat the milk and butter together in a saucepan over a low heat until the butter is completely melted and then add to the rest of the batter. Mix until fully combined and then pour the batter into the prepared baking dish.

Make the sauce by pouring the boiling water onto the sugar and cocoa powder. Mix to dissolve the sugar and then whisk in the Irish cream liqueur. Pour over the cake batter.

Bake for 30–35 minutes until the surface looks firm and crisp. Remove from the oven and dust with sifted icing sugar. Serve straight away with some cream.

BANANA AND CHOCOLATE BREAD AND BUTTER PUDDING

Prep Time 30–40 minutes + 3 hours chilling

Cook Time 30–35 minutes

Serves 8–10

Type of banana: YELLOW

Nut Free

---

8 slices medium-cut white bread

150g (5¼oz) dark chocolate

75g (2¾oz) salted butter

370ml (1½ cups) single cream

110g (4oz) caster sugar

½ tsp ground cinnamon

3 large eggs

2 bananas, thinly sliced, plus extra to serve

Ice cream, to serve

Remove the crusts from the bread and cut the slices into triangles.

Place the chocolate, butter, cream, sugar and cinnamon in a bowl and place over a pan of simmering water (make sure the water doesn't touch the bowl). Stir occasionally and remove from the heat when the chocolate and butter have melted and the sugar has dissolved. Stir the chocolate mix until fully combined, shiny and smooth.

In a separate bowl, whisk the eggs together. Pour the chocolate mix over the eggs while whisking. Keep whisking until everything is combined.

Pour around a 1cm (½in) depth of chocolate mix in the base of a 28cm (11in) long oval heatproof dish. Arrange half of the bread on top of the chocolate and then add the banana slices. Pour half of the remaining chocolate on top of this and then top with the remaining bread.

Finish with the remaining chocolate and then use a fork to push the bread down so it is evenly covered in liquid. Cover the dish with clingfilm and chill in the fridge for a minimum of 3 hours.

Preheat the oven to 180°C/160°C fan/350°F/Gas 4.

Remove the clingfilm from the dish and bake for 30–35 minutes. The top will be crunchy and the middle will be soft. Allow to cool for 10 minutes before serving with extra sliced banana and ice cream.

BANOFFEE TRIFLE

Prep Time 15–20 minutes + 1 hour cooling

Cook Time 5–10 minutes

Serves 4

Type of banana: YELLOW

Nut Free

200g (7oz) sponge fingers or ready-made sponge cake, sliced
4 tbsps brandy
2 bananas, sliced
250g (8¾oz) ready-made vanilla custard
5 tbsps double cream

FOR THE TOFFEE SAUCE
50g (1¾oz) salted butter
Pinch of salt
50g (1¾oz) light brown sugar
3 tbsps double cream

TO DECORATE
Chocolate shavings
Banana chips or slices

To make the toffee sauce, place the butter, salt and sugar in a saucepan and bring to the boil over a medium–low heat. Whisk constantly to make sure it doesn't burn on the bottom. Boil for around 15 seconds and then remove from the heat and slowly add the cream while whisking. Be careful at this stage as the toffee can spit.

Set aside to cool. The cooled toffee sauce should be pourable but not set.

Evenly layer half of the sponge fingers or sponge cake into a trifle bowl, then spoon over 2 tablespoons of the brandy. Pour half of the toffee sauce over the sponge, pushing it against the side of the dish to seal in the sponge below. Then add a layer of sliced banana. Pour over half of the custard, then repeat the layers. Put in the fridge to set for 1 hour.

Whip the double cream to soft peaks and top the trifle with it. Arrange some chocolate shavings and banana chips or slices over the top and then enjoy.

Tip: You can use ready-made toffee sauce if you wish; it will still be tasty.

EASY BANANA CHOCOLATE ICE CREAM

Prep Time 10–15 minutes + 3 hours freezing

Serves 3–4

Type of banana: BROWN

Gluten Free | Nut Free

---

4 bananas, mashed
3–4 tbsps full-fat milk
2 tbsps cocoa powder
100ml (3½ fl oz) whipping cream
45g (1½oz) icing sugar

Blend the bananas with the milk and cocoa powder until smooth.

In a separate bowl, whip the cream and sifted icing sugar together until you get stiff peaks.

Fold the banana mixture into the cream until smooth and then place all of the mixture into an airtight container. Place the container in the freezer for 1 hour and then thoroughly mix.

Return to the freezer for another 1 hour, then mix thoroughly. Repeat this freezing and mixing once more.

Tip: To enjoy the ice cream at its best, remove from the freezer 5–10 minutes before serving. The ice cream can be kept for 1 month in the freezer.

BOOZY BANANA CHOCOLATE TRIFLE

Prep Time 30–35 minutes + 1 ½ hours chilling
Cook Time 5 minutes
Serves 4
Type of banana: YELLOW
Nut Free

---

5 tbsps double cream
200g (7oz) ready-made brownies
8 tbsps Irish cream liqueur
2 bananas, sliced, plus extra to decorate
250g (8¾oz) ready-made vanilla custard

FOR THE GANACHE
100ml (3½ fl oz) double cream
80g (2¾oz) dark chocolate

Whip the cream to soft peaks and set aside.

To make the ganache, heat the cream in a saucepan over a low heat until it just starts to simmer, making sure to keep whisking while it's heating so it doesn't catch. Once heated, pour over the chocolate and leave for about 20 seconds without stirring. Whisk together until smooth and shiny. Set aside.

Evenly layer half of the brownies into the trifle bowl, then spoon over 4 tablespoons Irish cream liqueur. Pour over half of the chocolate ganache, pushing it against the side of the dish to seal in the brownies below. Leave to set for 30 minutes.

When the chocolate ganache has set, layer over half of the sliced bananas. Pour over half of the custard. Repeat the layers with the rest of the brownies, Irish cream, chocolate ganache, bananas and custard. Top with the whipped cream then place in the fridge for at least 1 hour to fully set.

Before serving, slice extra bananas on top and then enjoy.

Tip: You could make your own brownies and custard, in place of the ready made, if you like.

BANOFFEE CHEESECAKE

Prep Time 20–25 minutes + 4 hours chilling

Cook Time 2 hours

Serves 10

Type of banana: YELLOW

Nut Free

FOR THE BASE
180g (6¼oz) digestive biscuits
60g (2oz) salted butter, melted

FOR THE CARAMEL SAUCE
50g (1¾oz) butter
50g (1¾oz) light brown sugar
50ml (1¾ fl oz) double cream

FOR THE FILLING
300g (10½oz) cream cheese
65g (2¼oz) caster sugar
3 tsps cornflour
2 eggs
1½ tsps vanilla extract
150g (5¼oz) crème fraîche
2 small bananas, mashed, plus 1 banana, sliced, to decorate

Preheat the oven to 180°C/160°C fan/350°F/Gas 4. Double wrap the outside of an 18cm (7in) cake tin in foil.

For the base, place the biscuits in a food processor and blend until the biscuits have been broken down into an even crumb texture.

Mix together the crushed biscuits and melted butter. Press into the base of the tin and chill for 10 minutes.

While the base is chilling, make the caramel sauce. Place the butter and sugar in a saucepan over a medium heat. Whisk continuously, making sure the bottom doesn't burn. Bring to the boil and then remove from the heat and whisk in the cream. Set aside to cool.

Beat the cream cheese with an electric mixer until soft. Add the sugar, cornflour, eggs, vanilla, crème fraîche and mashed bananas and beat until smooth.

Gently pour the mixture over the set biscuit base. Swirl two-thirds of the cooled caramel sauce into the creamy filling, saving the last third for serving.

Sit the cheesecake tin in a roasting tin. Pour very hot water into the roasting tin so that it reaches halfway up the sides of the cake tin.

Bake in the centre of the oven for 1 hour. Turn off the oven, without opening the door, and leave for 1 hour to set. Cool and then chill for at least 4 hours, ideally overnight.

Remove the cheesecake from the tin, decorate with sliced bananas and serve with the remaining caramel sauce.

Tip: You can use ready-made toffee sauce if you wish; it will still be tasty.

FUN FACT

Bananas are one of the most popular fruits in the world and their health benefits are vast. They are rich in potassium, various B vitamins, vitamin C, antioxidants and fibre.

EASY BANANA ICE CREAM

Prep Time 10–15 minutes + 3 hours freezing

Serves 3–4

Type of banana: BROWN

Gluten Free | Nut Free

---

4 bananas, mashed
3–4 tbsps full-fat milk
100ml (3½ fl oz) whipping cream
45g (1½oz) icing sugar

In a blender, blend the bananas with the milk until smooth.

In a separate bowl, whip the cream and sifted icing sugar together until you get stiff peaks.

Fold the banana mixture into the cream until smooth and then place all of the mixture in an airtight container. Place the container in the freezer for 1 hour and then thoroughly mix.

Return to the freezer for another 1 hour, then mix thoroughly. Repeat this freezing and mixing once more and then enjoy!

Tip: To enjoy the ice cream like a soft serve, remove it from the freezer 5–10 minutes before serving. The ice cream can be kept for 1 month in the freezer.

BANANA AND RASPBERRY ICE CREAM CHEESECAKE

Prep Time 30–35 minutes + 3 hours freezing

Serves 8–10

Type of banana: YELLOW

Nut Free | Gluten Free

FOR THE BASE
150g (5¼oz) porridge oats
1 tbsp golden syrup
60g (2oz) butter, melted

FOR THE FILLING
3 small bananas, frozen
100g (3½oz) caster sugar
200g (7oz) cream cheese
2 tsps vanilla extract
Handful of raspberries

FOR THE COMPOTE
100g (3½oz) raspberries
2 tbsps granulated sugar
1 tsp vanilla extract

Grease a 20cm (8in) round loose-bottom tin.

Remove the bananas from the freezer and set aside.

To make the base, toast the oats in a large frying pan over a medium heat for about 5 minutes until they just start to turn golden brown, stirring all the time. Place them in a food processor and blend to a fine crumb. Add the golden syrup and melted butter and blend again until it clumps together.

Pour the mixture into the prepared tin and, using the back of a spoon, press into the base and around 2.5cm (1in) up the side of the tin. Put the base in the fridge while you make the filling.

To make the filling, put the slightly defrosted bananas into a food processor with the sugar, cream cheese and vanilla, then blend until you have a soft-scoop ice-cream texture. Spoon half the filling on top of the prepared base. Sprinkle a handful of raspberries on top and then spoon the rest of the filling on top of the raspberries and smooth over.

Place in the freezer for 3 hours. When you are ready to serve, make the compote by adding the raspberries, sugar and vanilla to a saucepan and stirring over a medium heat until the raspberries have just softened. This should only take a few minutes.

Take the cheesecake out of the freezer, slide it out of the cake tin and place on a serving dish. Add the warm compote on top and leave for a few minutes before slicing and enjoying.

Tip: You can make the compote a day in advance and keep it chilled in the fridge until serving. If you are freezing overnight, remove the cheesecake from the freezer 10–15 minutes before serving.

BANANA MASCARPONE TART

Prep Time 30–35 minutes
Serves 8–10
Type of banana: YELLOW
Gluten Free | Nut Free

FOR THE BASE
200g (7oz) dates
3 tbsps boiling water
100g (3½oz) porridge oats, plus extra to decorate (optional)

FOR THE FILLING
500g (1lb) mascarpone
1 banana, plus 1 banana, diced, to decorate
Juice of 1 lemon, plus the zest to decorate
150g (5¼oz) icing sugar

For the base, line a 20cm (8in) springform tin with clingfilm.

Roughly chop the dates and then soak them in the boiling water for 10 minutes. Add the dates and their soaking water, and the porridge oats to a blender and blend until it forms a mostly smooth ball. Press this into the prepared tin, evenly pressing it up the sides and base. Place this in the fridge to set while you make mascarpone filling.

For the filling, beat the mascarpone with an electric mixer for around 2 minutes until fluffy.

In a separate bowl, using a stick blender, blend the banana until it is a smooth paste. Add the lemon juice and icing sugar to the banana and mix until smooth. Add the banana mixture to the mascarpone and beat until fully combined. Spread the filling on to the chilled base and then decorate the edges of the tart with the diced banana, lemon zest and extra oats, if you like.

Tip: If you are not eating the tart straight away the banana decoration may go brown. To stop this, squeeze a generous amount of lemon juice over the diced banana before putting it on the tart.

BANANA AND CUSTARD TART

Prep Time 1 hour + 2 hours chilling

Cook Time 35–40 minutes

Serves 8–10

Type of banana: YELLOW

Nut Free

FOR THE PASTRY

60g (2oz) caster sugar

1 egg white

120g (4¼oz) salted butter

180g (6¼oz) plain flour, plus extra for dusting

FOR THE FILLING

275ml (9 fl oz) full-fat milk

110ml (3¾ fl oz) double cream

80g (2¾oz) granulated sugar

¼ tsp salt

2 egg yolks

2½ tbsps cornflour

1 tbsp vanilla extract

25g (1oz) salted butter, softened

3 bananas

To make the pastry, mix together the sugar and egg white in a large bowl until the sugar has mostly dissolved. Add the butter and flour and knead until it forms a smooth dough. Flatten the dough slightly and then wrap in clingfilm. Place the dough in the fridge for around 45 minutes.

Remove the dough from the fridge and roll out on a well-floured surface to around 1cm (½in) thickness. Line a deep, round 20cm (8in) tin with the pastry, letting any excess hang over the edge of the tin. Place this in the fridge for 10 minutes.

Preheat the oven to 200°C/180°C fan/400°F/Gas 6. Remove the pastry case from the fridge, line the inside of the pastry with baking parchment and fill to the top with baking beads.

Blind bake the pastry case for 20 minutes until the pastry holds its shape. Remove the beads and baking parchment and bake for a further 5 minutes to give the pastry some colour. Remove from the oven and trim off any excess pastry while it is still hot and then set aside to cool.

For the filling, add the milk, cream, sugar and salt to a saucepan over a medium heat. Whisk the ingredients until the sugar has dissolved.

Bring the mix to a simmer, whisking occasionally to stop it from burning. Once the milk mix starts to simmer, remove from the heat.

In a heatproof bowl, whisk together the egg yolks, cornflour and vanilla until smooth. Slowly pour around 100ml (3 ½ fl oz) of the milk mix into the eggs while continually whisking. Once fully combined, slowly pour the egg mix back into the pan, continually whisking again

Continued overleaf

(this stage is to stop the eggs from scrambling). Place the pan back over the heat and cook for around 1 minute until thick and large bubbles rise to the top when it's boiling, making sure to whisk the mixture.

Pour the custard into a heatproof dish and add the butter. Roughly chop one banana and add this to the custard as well. Using a hand blender, blend the custard until smooth. Place clingfilm directly on top of the custard to stop a skin from forming and allow to cool for around 25 minutes

While the custard is cooling, thinly slice 1 banana and then arrange it over the cooled pastry base.

Pour the custard over the banana and smooth the surface. Place the tart in the fridge for around 1 hour.

For the decoration, cut the remaining banana into 1cm (½in) cubes and then arrange the cubed banana around the rim of the tart and enjoy!

Tip: If you are not eating the tart straight away then the banana decoration may go brown. To stop this, squeeze a generous amount of lemon juice over the cubed banana before placing it on the tart.

SAVOURY
DISHES

CHICKEN AND BANANA KORMA

Prep Time 20–25 minutes

Cook Time 55–60 minutes

Serves 4–5

Type of banana: YELLOW

Gluten Free

---

1 brown onion, roughly chopped

1 red chilli, deseeded

5cm (2in) piece fresh root ginger, peeled and chopped

3 garlic cloves

2 tbsps sunflower oil

1 tbsp garam masala

2 tsps ground turmeric

450ml (15 fl oz) chicken stock

55g (2oz) ground almonds

4 skinless, boneless chicken thighs

150g (5¼oz) plain yogurt

2 tsps cornflour

2 large bananas

Handful of chopped fresh coriander, plus extra to garnish

Basmati or pilau rice, to serve

Place the onion, chilli, ginger and garlic in a food processor and process to a smooth purée. Heat the oil in a large non-stick pan and fry the onion mixture over a low-medium heat for about 10 minutes, stirring frequently to prevent it from sticking. Add the garam masala and turmeric and mix. Pour in the stock and stir in the ground almonds.

Add the chicken thighs to the pan. Cover and leave to simmer gently for 40 minutes, occasionally stirring to stop the bottom from burning.

Mix the yogurt and cornflour together. Add to the curry and simmer, stirring constantly, until thickened. Slice the bananas, then add to the curry with the chopped coriander. Cook for a few more minutes to warm the bananas.

Serve the curry with basmati or pilau rice and sprinkle generously with extra chopped coriander.

Tip: If you are serving vegetarians, simply omit the chicken and use vegetable stock.

RED THAI BANANA CURRY

Prep Time 15–20 minutes
Cook Time 50–55 minutes
Serves 4–6
Type of banana: GREEN
Dairy Free | Gluten Free

---

2 bananas
3 tsps coconut oil
60g (2oz) roasted salted cashews
140g (5oz) tinned chickpeas, drained and rinsed
4 skinless, boneless chicken thighs
1 red onion, chopped
2 garlic cloves, crushed
1 tbsp grated fresh root ginger
2 tbsps red Thai curry paste
400ml (1⅔ cups) water
1 vegetable stock cube
160ml (⅔ cup) coconut milk
2 tbsps soy sauce
40g (1½oz) sugar snap peas
Salt, to taste
Rice or flatbread, to serve

Slice the bananas into 1cm (½in) thick rounds.

Heat 1 teaspoon of the coconut oil in a large wok over a medium–high heat and add the banana. Cook until lightly browned, about 3 minutes on each side. Remove the banana and set aside.

Add another 1 teaspoon of the coconut oil to the wok. Add the cashews and chickpeas and cook until lightly browned, about 3 minutes. Remove from the wok and set aside.

Lower the heat to medium, and heat the remaining 1 teaspoon of coconut oil in the wok. Add the chicken, onion, garlic, ginger and curry paste, stirring until the chicken has browned on both sides.

Add the water, stock cube, coconut milk, soy sauce, chickpeas and cashew nuts. Cook for 30–35 minutes until the chicken is cooked through. Add the banana and cook for a further 5 minutes. Taste and add salt to your liking.

Top with the sugar snap peas and serve with rice or flatbread.

Tip: This recipe can be easily made for vegetarians by leaving out the chicken.

FUN FACT

Bananas are eaten across the world and in so many ways. They are commonly used in savoury dishes to create a beautiful balance of sweet and savoury, from hot banana soup in Puerto Rico to roast bananas and pork in Peru.

BANANA AND POTATO SOUP

Prep Time 20–25 minutes
Cook Time 50 minutes–1 hour
Serves 3–4
Type of banana: GREEN
Gluten Free | Nut Free

---

2 bananas
15g (½oz) salted butter
1 brown onion, chopped
2 garlic cloves, crushed
2 tsps paprika
2 tsps ground coriander
1 tsp ground cumin
500ml (2 cups) water
1 vegetable stock cube
2 tbsps lime juice
300g (10½oz) potatoes, peeled and cubed (equivalent
 of 2 potatoes)
Salt, to taste
Fresh coriander, to garnish
Warm fresh bread, to serve

Slice the bananas into 2cm (¾in) rounds.

Melt the butter in a pan and sweat the onion and garlic for 5 minutes over a low heat. Stir in the paprika, ground coriander and cumin and cook for about 30 seconds. Add the water, stock cube, bananas, lime juice and salt to taste.

Bring to the boil. Cover and simmer gently for 15 minutes.

Process the soup in a blender and return to the pan.

Add the potatoes and simmer for 25-30 minutes or until they are tender.

Check seasonings and add salt if required. Serve with a garnish of coriander and warm fresh bread.

GREEN BANANA SOUP

Prep Time 10–15 minutes
Cook Time 30–35 minutes
Serves 3–4
Type of banana: GREEN
Dairy Free | Nut Free | Vegan

---

4 bananas
2 tbsps coconut oil
2 red onions, finely chopped
2 garlic cloves, finely chopped
1 tsp ground turmeric
1 tsp ground cumin
2 tsps ground coriander
1 tsp smoked paprika
4 medium tomatoes, skinned and diced
100g (3½oz) spinach
2 carrots, peeled and diced
1 vegetable stock cube
600ml (2½ cups) water
Handful of chopped fresh coriander (optional)
Salt and black pepper, to taste
Bread, to serve

Diagonally slice the bananas into 3cm (1½in) thick pieces and set aside.

Heat the coconut oil in a saucepan over a medium heat and fry the onion, garlic and all the spices for 5 minutes. Keep stirring to avoid burning the spices.

When the onions are softened add the diced tomato, spinach, carrot, stock cube and water. Season with salt and pepper to your liking.

Simmer with the lid on for around 20–25 minutes until the carrots are tender. Add the banana slices and cook for a further 5 minutes.

Stir through a handful of chopped coriander, if you like, and serve with your favourite bread.

GREEN BANANA FRIES

Prep Time 5–10 minutes
Cook Time 10–15 minutes
Serves 3 as a side
Type of banana: GREEN
Dairy Free | Gluten Free | Nut Free | Vegan

---

3 bananas
Vegetable oil, for frying
Salt, to taste

Peel and slice the bananas into thin fries.

Half fill a heavy pan with oil. Heat the oil over a medium–high heat. Once the oil is hot (around 190°C/375°F), carefully place the banana fries into the hot oil and fry until golden brown, around 10–15 minutes.

Remove from the oil, place on paper towels and pat to drain off any excess oil. Season with salt and serve immediately.

FUN FACT

Another variety of banana is the cooking banana, commonly known as plantain. Plantain is a staple in central America, West and Central Africa and the Caribbean Islands.

TATALE (PLANTAIN PANCAKES)

Prep Time 10 minutes + 25 minutes resting

Cook Time 15–20 minutes

Makes 4–5 as a side

Type of banana: BLACK PLANTAIN

Dairy Free | Nut Free | Vegan

---

2 plantains
1 small brown onion, finely chopped
½ tsp grated fresh root ginger
¼ tsp chilli flakes
1 tsp salt
70g (2½oz) plain flour
Vegetable oil, for frying

Mash the plantain until mostly smooth (you can use a hand blender to help). Stir in the chopped onion, grated ginger, chilli flakes and salt.

Add the flour and stir until fully combined and then allow the mixture to rest for around 25 minutes.

After resting, heat a shallow layer of oil in a non-stick frying pan over a medium heat. Add around 2 tablespoons of mixture to the pan and then flatten this slightly to make a round patty. Fry the pancake for around 2 minutes on each side or until it is a dark golden colour. Keep warm and repeat until all of the mixture has been used.

Enjoy as a snack or as a side with stew and hot sauce.

Tip: Use very, very ripe plantain with skins that are almost completely black. You can add more chilli flakes to the recipe if you prefer a bit of a kick!

BAKED PLANTAIN CHIPS

Prep Time 5 minutes

Cook Time 35 minutes

Serves 4 as a snack

Type of banana: YELLOW

Dairy Free | Gluten Free | Nut Free | Vegan

---

4 plantains
2 tbsps sunflower oil
Salt, to taste

Preheat the oven to 220°C/200°C fan/425°F/Gas 7.

Slice the plantains very thinly and then place them in a bowl. Pour in the oil, sprinkle the salt over the plantains and give them a good stir.

Once the oil has been evenly distributed, place the slices on a baking tray lined with baking parchment, in one layer.

Bake for 12–15 minutes, flipping the chips halfway through. When each chip is slightly golden around the edge, switch off the oven. Leave the chips in the oven for a further 20 minutes. Remove from the oven and allow to cool completely on the tray. Sprinkle with additional salt if required and enjoy.

Tip: These chips are crispiest on the day they are made but, if you don't get through them, they will keep for another day in an airtight container.

BANANA PEEL CRACKLING

Prep Time 25 minutes
Cook Time 30–35 minutes
Makes 24
Type of banana: YELLOW
Dairy Free | Gluten Free | Nut Free | Vegan

---

4 bananas
2 tsps salt
2 tsps smoked paprika
Pinch of black pepper
Pinch of caster sugar
Vegetable oil, for frying

Thoroughly wash the bananas to remove any bitter residue from the peel. Remove the peel from the bananas in 3 long strands. Cut off the ends and then scrape off the white inside of the peel with a spoon. Cut each length in half and soak them in cold water for 10 minutes. Drain and dry the peel on some paper towel.

While the peel is soaking, mix together the salt, paprika, pepper and sugar in a bowl and set aside.

Fill a heavy saucepan one-third full with oil and then heat to 195°C (380°F) over a low–medium heat. Add a couple slices of peel at a time to give the oil time to heat back up after each addition. Fry the peel for around 3–5 minutes until golden brown. Place on some paper towel to drain off any excess oil and then immediately sprinkle with some of the mixed seasoning. Repeat with all the peel and then enjoy.

Tip: These are best on the day they are made.

RED PEPPER AND CHORIZO MUFFINS

Prep Time 10–15 minutes

Cook Time 15–20 minutes

Makes 12

Type of banana: GREEN

Nut Free

---

1 small banana
5 tbsps olive oil
4 eggs
200ml (6¾ fl oz) full-fat milk
70g (2½oz) red pepper, cut into 1cm (½in) cubes
100g (3½oz) chorizo, cut into 1cm (½in) cubes
40g (1½oz) Cheddar, grated
¼ tsp paprika
2 tsps salt
425g (15oz) self-raising flour
2 tsps baking powder
Handful of pumpkin seeds

Preheat the oven to 200°C/180°C fan/350°F/Gas 6. Line a 12-hole muffin tray with muffin cases.

Using a stick blender, blend the banana with 1 tablespoon of olive oil until smooth. Mix the purée with the eggs, milk and remaining olive oil.

Add the chopped pepper, chorizo, cheese, paprika, salt, flour and baking powder and mix until fully combined.

Divide the mixture evenly between the 12 muffin cases and then sprinkle the pumpkin seeds on top.

Bake the muffins for 15–20 minutes until a skewer comes out clean when the muffin is poked.

Tip: These muffins are best eaten within 2 days of being baked. Keep them in an airtight container to help them retain their freshness. If you want to make this recipe suitable for vegetarians, you can swap the chorizo for red onion.

BBQ PULLED BANANA PEEL

Prep Time 25 minutes
Cook Time 25–30 minutes
Serves 4–5
Type of banana: YELLOW
Dairy Free | Gluten Free | Nut Free | Vegan

---

3 tsps cornflour
3 tsps smoked paprika
Pinch of black pepper
2 tsps garlic powder
3 tsps dried parsley
4 bananas
2 tbsps water
½ tsp salt
Vegetable oil, for frying

TO SERVE
4–5 gluten-free bread buns (optional)
Your favourite toppings, for example lettuce, tomato, coleslaw

Mix together the salt, cornflour, paprika, pepper, garlic powder and parsley in a dish and set aside for later.

Thoroughly wash the bananas to remove any bitter residue or pesticides from the peel. Remove the peel from the bananas in 3 long strands. Cut off the ends and then scrape off the white material on the inside with a spoon. Cut each length in half and then into very thin strands.

Bring a pan of water to the boil and add the strands of peel. Boil the peel for 20 minutes and then drain. Tip the peel into the dish with the spices and give it a good stir to make sure all the strands are evenly coated.

Heat a small amount of oil in a non-stick frying pan over medium–high heat. Once the oil is hot, add the peel and fry for around 1–2 minutes until each strand starts to brown all over.

Add the water and boil for around 1 minute until all the peel is covered in a sticky sauce.

Serve on bread buns with your favourite toppings.

Tip: The best bananas to use for this recipe are yellow ones that are starting to get some brown spots.

ONION AND BANANA BHAJIS

Prep Time 10–15 minutes

Cook Time 30–40 minutes

Makes 18–20 small bhajis

Type of banana: YELLOW

Dairy Free | Gluten Free | Nut Free | Vegan

---

2 large brown onions, finely sliced
100g (3½oz) gram flour
½ tsp gluten-free baking powder
½ tsp ground cumin
½ tsp ground turmeric
2 green chillies, finely chopped
1 banana, mashed
100ml (3½ fl oz) cold water
Salt, to taste
Vegetable oil, for frying

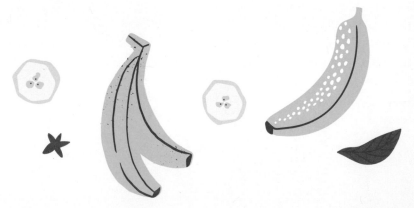

Soak the finely sliced onions in cold water while you make the batter.

Sift the flour and baking powder into a large bowl. Add the cumin, turmeric and 1 teaspoon salt and stir the dry ingredients together. Add the chillies and banana with the cold water. Stir together until you get a thick batter.

Drain the onions well and add them to the batter. Stir the mix until the onions are evenly coated in batter and then set aside while you heat the oil.

Heat around 5cm (2in) of oil in a heavy saucepan over a low heat; do not fill the pan more than a third full. You can test if the oil is the right temperature by dropping a tiny amount of batter into the oil. If it sizzles and begins to rise to the surface after 30 seconds, it is ready.

Carefully lower large tablespoons of the mixture into the oil, frying a couple at a time. Fry the bhajis for around 3–4 minutes until they are evenly golden brown. You may need to flip them halfway through cooking to get that even golden brown colour. Once cooked, place them on paper towels to drain off any excess oil and keep warm while you cook the rest. Sprinkle the bhajis with salt and enjoy them fresh.

Tip: These bhajis are best eaten fresh but they can be reheated in the oven at 200°C/180°C fan/350°F/Gas 6 for 5–10 minutes. Make sure they are piping hot before eating.

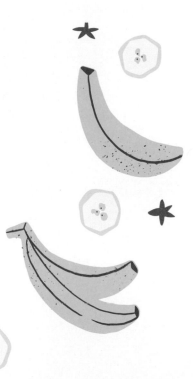

Although there is no botanical difference between bananas and plantains, the name plantain is loosely given to a type of banana that is cooked before it is eaten. Plantains are also larger and firmer than the standard banana.

FRIED PLANTAIN

Prep Time 5 minutes

Cook Time 5 minutes

Serves 2 as a snack or side

Type of banana: BLACK PLANTAIN

Dairy Free | Gluten Free | Nut Free | Vegan

---

2 plantains
3 tbsps vegetable oil, for frying
Salt, to taste

Diagonally slice the plantain into 2cm (¾in) thick pieces.

Fill the bottom of a frying pan with oil 1cm (½in) deep and place over a medium heat. When the oil is hot enough (it should sizzle), start frying the plantain in batches so that the oil doesn't cool down too much. Fry the plantain on each side for around 1–1½ minutes or until golden brown.

Once golden, place on paper towels to dry off any excess oil. Sprinkle with salt and enjoy.

Tip: The best plantains for frying are ones that are mostly black; they have the best and sweetest flavour. Fried plantain can be eaten as a snack or as a side to some stew and rice. Either way, it is a delicious sweet and salty treat.

CURRIED BANANA CHUTNEY

Prep Time 5–10 minutes

Cook Time 1 hour

Makes 6 small jars

Type of banana: YELLOW

Dairy Free | Gluten Free | Nut Free | Vegan

---

4 large bananas, sliced

1 green pepper, deseeded and finely chopped

2 red onions, finely chopped

100g (3½oz) cauliflower, chopped

2 garlic cloves, finely chopped

2 tsps salt

Pinch of ground black pepper

1 tsp mild curry powder

1 tsp ground turmeric

¼ tsp dried thyme

¼ tsp ground cumin

360ml (1½ cups) white wine vinegar

100g (3½oz) granulated sugar

Stir all the ingredients together in a saucepan over a low heat and simmer for 1 hour. Stir occasionally to make sure the chutney doesn't stick to the bottom of the pan.

Halfway through the cooking process, start sterilizing the jars. Preheat the oven to 160°C/140°C fan/320°F/Gas 3. While the oven is heating, wash the jars and lids in hot, soapy water and leave them to drain dry (do not dry with a tea towel or cloth). Always wash a few extra in case. Place the drained jars and lids on a baking tray and then heat for a minimum of 15 minutes.

Switch off the oven and, once the chutney is cooked, take the jars out of the oven. Bottle the chutney into the hot jars, leaving around 0.5cm (¼in) at the top of the jars. Screw on the lids and then allow to cool. Allow the chutney to mature for at least 3 days before digging in.

Tip: It is important to bottle the chutney when both the chutney and the jars are still hot to give it the best chance at a long shelf life. Some curry powders can be contaminated with gluten or nuts, so double check before making this recipe for anyone with allergies. The chutney can last unopened for at least 6 months when kept in a cool, dark place.

SPICED BANANA AND LIME RELISH

Prep Time 10–15 minutes

Cook Time 30–35 minutes

Makes 4 small jars

Type of banana: GREEN

Dairy Free | Gluten Free | Nut Free | Vegan

---

3 tbsps vegetable oil

2 brown onions, finely chopped

2 garlic cloves, chopped

3 green chillies, deseeded and finely chopped

Zest and juice of 3 limes

2 tsps ground turmeric

1 tsp mustard powder

2 tomatoes, finely chopped

1 tbsp light brown sugar

2½ tbsps white wine vinegar

2 bananas, diced

1 tsp salt

1 small bunch of fresh coriander, chopped

Preheat the oven to 160°C/140°C fan/320°F/Gas 3.

While the oven is heating, wash your jars and lids in hot, soapy water and leave them to drain dry (do not dry with a tea towel or cloth). Always wash a couple extra jars in case. Place the drained jars and lids on a baking tray and then heat them while you make the relish.

Heat the oil in a large frying pan over a low heat. Add the onion, garlic, chilli and lime zest and fry for around 10 minutes or until the onions have softened. Add the turmeric, mustard powder and tomatoes and cook for around 5 minutes to soften the tomatoes. Add the sugar and vinegar and stir until the sugar has dissolved. Stir in the banana and cook for a further 5 minutes. Add the lime juice, salt and coriander and cook for 15 minutes.

Once the relish is cooked, take the jars out of the oven. Bottle the chutney into the hot jars, leaving a 0.5cm (¼in) space at the top of the jars. Screw on the lids and then allow to cool.

Tip: It is important to put the relish in jars when both the relish and the jars are still hot to give it the best chance at a long shelf life. This delicious relish can be kept unopened for 6 months in a cool, dark place.

CHICKEN AND BANANA SATAY

Prep Time 10–15 minutes

Cook Time 1 hour 5 minutes

Serves 4–5

Type of banana: GREEN

Dairy Free | Gluten Free

---

3 tbsps vegetable oil
4 skinless chicken pieces
1 tsp ground cumin
2 tsps ground coriander
½ tsp ground ginger
1 tsp paprika
1 onion, finely chopped
1 red pepper, deseeded and chopped
2 garlic cloves, minced
180g (6¼oz) smooth peanut butter
1 x 400g (14oz) tin chopped tomatoes
1 vegetable stock cube
1 large banana
Salt, to taste
Rice, to serve

Heat the oil in a large saucepan over a medium–high heat. Add the chicken, cumin, coriander, ginger and paprika. Fry the chicken for around 10 minutes until it is golden, then remove the chicken from the pan.

Turn the heat down to low–medium and then add the onion, red pepper and garlic. Fry for around 5 minutes or until the onions have softened. Add the peanut butter and fry this for a further 5 minutes, stirring constantly, to soften the peanut butter and allow the oils to come out.

Add the chopped tomatoes in stages, stirring vigorously in between. This is to stop the peanut butter from separating from the sauce. Fill the tomato tin with water and add this to the pan as well. Stir in the stock cube and the fried chicken. Simmer for 45 minutes, stirring often to make sure the sauce doesn't stick. In the last 10 minutes of cooking, slice the banana and add it to the sauce. Add salt to taste and enjoy with rice.

Tip: This recipe is loosely based on Ghanaian groundnut stew and is usually cooked with Scotch bonnet peppers. I like to add hot sauce to my own portion but you can add as much chilli as you want to the recipe.

DRINKS

TROPICAL SMOOTHIE

Prep Time 5 minutes

Serves 2

Type of banana: YELLOW

Dairy Free | Gluten Free | Nut Free | Vegan

Juice of 2 oranges
Juice of 1 grapefruit
1 banana, roughly chopped
125ml (½ cup) coconut water
3 tbsps agave syrup
½ tsp vanilla extract

Blend the orange and grapefruit
juices with the banana until
smooth. Add the coconut water,
syrup and vanilla and blend
till completely mixed and then
enjoy fresh.

Tip: Enjoy this smoothie straight away or it can be kept in the fridge
for 1 day if you need to make it in advance.

BERRY SMOOTHIE

Prep Time 5 minutes

Serves 1–2

Type of banana: YELLOW

Dairy Free | Gluten Free | Nut Free | Vegan

---

1 banana, roughly chopped
30g (1oz) blueberries
75g (2¾oz) strawberries
150ml (5 fl oz) apple juice
2 tbsps golden syrup

Blend all the
ingredients
together until
smooth and enjoy.

Tips: You can replace the apple juice with oat milk to get a creamier texture. Enjoy straight away or it can be kept in the fridge for 1 day.

WAKE UP SMOOTHIE BOWL

Prep Time 5 minutes

Serves 2

Type of banana: YELLOW

Dairy Free | Gluten Free | Nut Free | Vegan

---

2 bananas, roughly chopped
100g (3½oz) berries, such as strawberries, blueberries or raspberries
2 apples, cored
6 tbsps apple juice
4 tbsps golden syrup

TO SERVE
1 tbsp oats
Slices of your favourite fruit

Blend the banana, berries, apples, apple juice and golden syrup together until smooth.

Serve in bowls, topped with the oats and slices of your favourite fruit.

Tip: This smoothie bowl is best enjoyed straight away but it can be kept in the fridge for 1 day.

FUN FACT

Because bananas are such a good source of high-energy carbohydrates, they are popular among athletes and are also ideal for active, growing children.

BANANA AND COCONUT COCKTAIL

Prep Time 5 minutes

Serves 3–4

Type of banana: YELLOW

Dairy Free | Gluten Free | Nut Free | Vegan

---

2 bananas, roughly chopped
50ml (2 fl oz) coconut milk
4 tbsps agave syrup
Juice of ½ lime
200ml (6¾ fl oz) coconut water
100ml (3½ fl oz) coconut rum
Lime wedges, to garnish (optional)

Blend the banana, coconut milk, syrup and lime juice until smooth. Add the coconut water and rum and stir to fully mix.

Evenly divide the drink between cocktail glasses and garnish each with a lime wedge, if you like.

BANANA DAIQUIRI

Prep Time 5 minutes

Serves 1–2

Type of banana: YELLOW

Dairy Free | Gluten Free | Nut Free | Vegan

100ml (3½ fl oz) light rum
50ml (2 fl oz) triple sec
1 banana, mashed
2 tbsps sugar syrup
150ml (5 fl oz) lime juice
1 tsp granulated sugar
30g (1oz) crushed ice
Lime twists, to garnish (optional)

Add all the ingredients to a shaker filled with ice cubes and shake until well chilled.

Strain into a chilled cocktail glass and garnish with a lime twist, if you like.

BANANA MOJITO

Prep Time 5 minutes

Serves 1

Type of banana: BANANA LIQUEUR

Dairy Free | Gluten Free | Nut Free | Vegan

---

2 tbsps banana liqueur
10 mint leaves, plus extra to garnish
150ml (5 fl oz) light rum
50ml (2 fl oz) soda water
Juice of 1 lime

Add all the ingredients to a shaker filled with ice cubes and shake until well chilled. Strain into cocktail glasses and garnish with a lime wedge and some fresh mint leaves.

GREEN SMOOTHIE

Prep Time 5 minutes

Serves 2–3

Type of banana: YELLOW

Dairy Free | Gluten Free | Nut Free | Vegan

---

2 bananas, roughly chopped
100g (3½oz) spinach
2 apples, cored
5 tbsps apple juice
1 tsp spirulina (optional)

Blend the banana, spinach,
apples, apple juice and spirulina,
if using, together until smooth
and then enjoy.

Tip: You can enjoy this smoothie straight away or it can be kept in
the fridge for 1 day.

BANANA SPLIT MARTINI

Prep Time 5 minutes
Serves 1
Type of banana: YELLOW
Gluten Free | Nut Free

150ml (5 fl oz) vodka
5 tbsps crème de banane or banana liqueur
5 tbsps crème de cacao

TO GARNISH
Banana slices
Glacé cherries
Whipped cream

Add all the ingredients to a shaker filled with ice cubes and shake until well chilled.

Strain into a cocktail glass and add any of suggested garnishes.

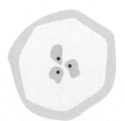

BANANA MILKSHAKE

Prep Time 5 minutes
Serves 2
Type of banana: YELLOW
Gluten Free | Nut Free

---

2 bananas, roughly chopped
50ml (2 fl oz) single cream
2 tbsps honey
1 tsp vanilla extract
150ml (5 fl oz) full-fat milk
Ice cream, to serve (optional)

Place the banana, cream and honey in a blender and blend until smooth. Add the vanilla and milk and blend until combined.

Serve chilled with a scoop of ice cream on top for some extra indulgence, if you like.

ACKNOWLEDGEMENTS

I would like to thank my mother for inspiring me to write this book and coming with me on my countless trips to the shops when I inevitably ran out of bananas. You even excitedly ate all of my experiments, no matter how dire. A massive thank you to my sister, Saara El-Arifi, for your encouragement and guidance with getting this book to where it is now.

Silé Edwards, the most incredible agent, for your unwavering support and never-ending excitement for bananas. To everyone at Mushens Entertainment for your positivity and giving me a massive confidence boost with every contact. To Nira Begum, Kate Fox and the whole HQ team for making this book a beautiful reality, and Steve Wells for making this reality beautiful with your wonderful designs.